EXERCISES IN THE HISTORY OF ENGLISH

Alan M. Markman
University of Pittsburgh

Erwin R. Steinberg
Carnegie-Mellon University

UNIVERSITY
PRESS OF
AMERICA

LANHAM • NEW YORK • LONDON

Copyright © 1970 by **Random House, Inc.**

(Originally published as Part Eight in *English: Then and Now*

by Alan M. Markman and Erwin R. Steinberg)

Copyright © 1983 by

University Press of America,® Inc.

4720 Boston Way
Lanham, MD 20706

3 Henrietta Street
London WC2E 8LU England

Printed in the United States of America

Library of Congress Cataloging in Publication Data

Markman, Alan M. (Alan Mouns), 1918-1970.
    Exercises in the history of English.

    Reprint. Originally published as pt. 8 in: English,
then and now. New York : Random House, [1970]
    Bibliography: p.
    1. English language—History—Problems, exercises,
etc.   2. Anglo-Saxon language—Texts.   3. English
language—Middle English, 1100-1500—Texts.   4.English
language—Early modern, 1500-1700—Texts.   I Steinberg,
Erwin Ray.   II. Title.
PE1075.5.M37   1983   420'.9   82-23769
ISBN 0-8191-2971-2

All University Press of America books are produced on acid-free
paper which exceeds the minimum standards set by the National
Historical Publications and Records Commission.

Part Eight   Exercises in the History of English

✠

INTRODUCTION

Millions of speakers of English today know nothing of the origin of their language, its relation to other languages, or its development over the course of some twelve hundred years. Yet, for the most part, they are fluent speakers; they carry out their day to day activities with apparent ease. Many of them write as well and about as comfortably as they speak. Most of our contemporary writers have had no formal training in, and little private inquiry into, the English language. It cannot be said, therefore, that a knowledge of the history and the development of one's native language will lead to practical results, will make one a better speaker or writer or reader or listener of contemporary English. On the contrary, we know perfectly well that competence and performance in language depend on continuous activity in those four linguistic skills, on engaging vigorously, from day to day, with or without formal training, in the most fundamental of all human and social activities, using language. If, therefore, it cannot be claimed that knowledge of the history and development of English will have any appreciable effect upon performance in that language, why, then, should one bother with it?

The easiest thing to say, of course, is that no one could read a text written in older English if some knowledge of the phonology, the morphology, and the syntax of English, at whatever date one chose to read it, were not available, if a grammar of that language were not constructed. Chaucer's Squire, who hoped "to stonden in his lady grace," would be totally irretrievable; Guinevere, speaking thus to Launcelot, "therefor, wyt thou wel I am sette in such a plyte to gete my soule hele," might be misunderstood by us; the *Authorized Version* rendering in Isaiah xiv:9–12, "O Lucifer, sonne of the morning? How art thou cut downe to the ground, which didst weaken the nations?" would strike us as non-English; Falstaff's curt order to Quickly to "wash thy face, and draw thy Action" might seem absurd; John Locke's judgment of the Greeks and their language ("On the Teaching of English") that "it is plain [they] were yet more nice in theirs" would be incomprehensible. Hundreds of examples, both earlier and later, could be strung out here, but there is little need for that. The point is clear: without instruction we could not read the texts our ancestors produced, we could not have access to the record and literature of the past. Since much of the glory and wisdom of humanity would on that account be lost to posterity, many of us would be inclined to say that the study of the history of our language, if it prevents that calamity, is indeed justified. But there is not likely to be an overwhelming majority of that persuasion among those for whom these exercises are intended.

If we set immediately practical considerations aside, however, we will be able to recognize the appeal of historical study of the type represented in these exercises. During the past few decades, because of the necessity for isolating what one "needs to know," many of us have altogether lost sight of the exciting area of human activity called "the nice to know." In our hurry to accomplish some limited goals we have come close to rushing right out of the world without ever having sampled the largest portion of experience in it. A major justification for studies in historical grammar—or grammar of any sort, for that matter—is the opportunity they afford for putting intellectual curiosity and a general power of analysis to work. One might then regard a problem in, say, Old English syntax, as a proper sphere of study in its own right, worthy of the most concentrated mental effort.

The qualities of mind exercised by engaging in research in historical linguistics are, among others, curiosity, analysis, and patience, all directed to a quest for knowledge for its own sake, its own (often private) reward. That is what the study of historical grammar has to offer—knowledge. What is asked for here is careful observation, collection, and classification of language data, plus the ability to draw out, at the end of that activity, sound inferences, or conclusions, which are supported rigorously by that data.

The purpose of the following exercises is to provide an introduction to the historical study of our language. While the information which can be accumulated as a result of working through these exercises is sound and valuable in itself, it is elementary and partial. Only one short drill in phonology, for example, has been included. And the syntactical elements, although, once again, quite sound, in no way constitute a thorough history of English syntax. But this book is not a text for an advanced course in the history of English; rather, it was designed as a set of readings and exercises to satisfy the initial curiosity of students in English language and literature classes who might be expected to have some interest in the history and development of their language.

PLAN OF THE EXERCISES

The pursuit of knowledge about the English language is best carried on by employing an inductive methodology. Only after a reasonably wide assortment of language data has been observed, assembled, and analyzed can we make valid generalizations about language. Those are the assumptions that inform the texts and questions constituting these exercises. In the best sense of it, these exercises are a "do-it-yourself" course in The History and Development of the English Language. Although a good deal of information has been supplied, each of you will arrive at a number of answers on your own; the collective force of your own answers will become your basic knowledge of the history of your language.

The arrangement of texts is chronological, from earliest to latest. While this ordering of material does impose difficulties at first, the sense of progression to be gained by following this order will, we think, more than offset any initial hardships you may encounter. Also, the greatest help is provided in the early exercises. By examining passages chosen to represent the four stages in the development of English (Old English = OE, Middle English = ME, Early Modern English = EMnE, and Modern English = MnE), one can gain a reasonably well informed opinion about the course of his language.

In each of the exercises there are texts and questions for you to answer. Frequently there is also a translation or some explanatory material (a glossary or notes—or both). The order in which these materials appear varies from exercise to exercise, depending upon what you are asked to do with them. When you undertake an exercise, therefore, you should first skim it from beginning to end so that you will know what help has been provided for you and what is being asked of you. You will then be able to proceed through the exercise with confidence.

A FEW FINAL WORDS

Although each set of texts and exercises constitutes a reasonably good self-contained unit of information, it would be prudent to consult from time to time a few of the many reference books and texts which contain information relevant to the development of the English language. Here is a very short list of useful books; the bibliographies and notes found in them can lead the curious even further.

1. *OED. The Oxford English Dictionary*. 13 vols. The original title of this work was *A New English Dictionary on Historical Principles (NED)*, but it is now universally called the *OED*. First on any list, this is the single most important book for the study of the development of English. It is also the best dictionary of its kind in the world. Abridged editions are available and may have to be used, but one should become familiar with the whole set and, especially, its prefatory material.

2. John Algeo and Thomas Pyles. *Problems in the Origins and Development of the English Language*. New York: Harcourt, Brace, and World, 1966. The very best workbook available, it is keyed to Pyles' book, q.v., below.

3. Albert C. Baugh. *A History of the English Language*. 2nd ed. New York: Appleton, Century, Croft 1957.

4. Morton W. Bloomfield and Leonard Newmark. *A Linguistic Introduction to the History of English*. New York: Random House, 1963.

5. W. Nelson Francis. *The English Language: An Introduction–Background for Writing.* New York: W. W. Norton Co., 1965.

6. H. A. Gleason, Jr. *Linguistics and English Grammar.* New York: Holt, Rinehart, Winston, 1965.

7. Albert H. Marckwardt. *Introduction to the English Language.* New York: Oxford University Press, 1942.

8. L. M. Meyers. *The Roots of Modern English.* Boston: Little, Brown & Co., 1966.

9. John Nist. *A Structural History of English.* New York: St. Martin's Press, 1966.

10. Thomas Pyles. *The Origins and Development of the English Language.* New York: Harcourt, Brace, & World, 1964.

11. Stuart Robertson and Frederic G. Cassidy. *The Development of Modern English.* 2nd ed. New York: Prentice-Hall, Inc., 1954.

Before letting you go off on your own, a bit of cautionary advice seems appropriate. It would be wise to keep that eighteenth-century dictum about 'a little knowledge' in mind. Do not expect to know everything about the development of English when you have finished these exercises. No one knows 'everything' about language. Large areas of study have not even been suggested here. Think, for example, of the condition of English at the present time, of the varieties of English spoken by native English speakers in Britain, in the United States, in Canada, in Australia, in New Zealand, and in many other countries in the world, and of the type of English being spoken and written by native speakers of other languages who have learned English as a second language in every country of the world, and of the opportunities for research and study regarding the future of English this situation presents. Much, therefore, is left to be examined. For further study, however, these exercises will furnish a decent foundation; and that is a sufficient beginning.

To make the following exercises more meaningful and informative, and to render meaningful the list of abbreviations and the glossary that appear in Exercise 1, we suggest examining this preliminary exercise and answering the questions in it.

PRELIMINARY EXERCISE

A sound view of the parts of speech and grammatical properties is essential in making accurate translations. Old English, as you will discover, is an inflected language, much closer, in this respect, to modern German than it is to Modern English. In MnE 'he did not say' is a grammatical sentence, but none of the following sentences is grammatical:

he not did say
not say he did
he not say did
not said he

and 'did he not say' is not equivalent. We test grammaticalness, in these instances, by relating each utterance to word order models we have learned. In OE, however, *ne sægde hē* (literally, word for word, equivalent to MnE '*not said he')* is grammatical and equivalent, in translation, to 'he did not say.' We are able to construct this equivalence in our translation by drawing on our knowledge of grammar, by realizing that OE word order is different from, and based on principles of organization which are different from, that of MnE. In this instance we need to know this much (at least) of OE grammar:

1. the negative particle *ne* (not) often appears initially in a negative sentence

2. as is the case in OE with an initial *þa* (*þa fērde hē*, then he travelled), after *ne* the verb almost always appears next, the subject appearing after the verb

3. the conjugation of the verb *secgan* (say) shows that *sægde* is third person singular preterite indicative (i.e., 'said,' with 'he,' 'she,' or 'it' as possible subjects)

4. as we contruct 'said' from 'say' we observe that we can place 'I,' 'you,' 'he,' or 'she,' and 'they' before it, but in OE, in an equivalent situation, 'I' and 'he' or 'she' would require *sægde*, 'you' would require *sægdest*, and 'they' would require *sægdon*. Thus the final -e of *sægde* carries with it a certain type of grammatical information not contained in its MnE equivalent, 'said.'

QUESTIONS

It might be helpful, in answering these questions, to consult a handbook or traditional description of MnE.

1. What is a grammatical property?
2. What is a part of speech? How many of them are there?
3. What does *gender* signify? How is it determined and recognized?
4. What does *number* signify? How is it determined and recognized?
5. What does *case* signify? How is it determined and recognized?
6. How many *cases* are there, in MnE, for nouns?
7. In verb constructions what does *number* signify? How is it determined and recognized? Wherein does it reside?
8. To what natural phenomenon does *tense* relate? How is it determined and recognized?
9. What is *mood*? How is it determined and recognized?
10. What is *concord* (or agreement)? Under what grammatical circumstances is it required? Why?

*Asterisk in front of a structure signifies that the structure is nongrammatical, not permitted in MnE.

11. What is a *declension*? a *conjugation*? a *paradigm*?

12. What is a *pro*-noun? What other *pro*-forms do you recognize in MnE? Under what grammatical circumstances can they occur?

13. Do you understand each of the definitions cited for the abbreviations listed in the glossary for Exercise 1 on pages 377–381?

14. After you complete this exercise, read "The Legend of St. Andrew," which follows. Answer the first twelve questions above as if they were directed to that OE text, and compare your answers with the responses you have just made. What differences show up?

✠ ✠ ✠

OLD ENGLISH
450–1154

It is not possible to fix the exact date of the earliest surviving Old English text. Perhaps the poem *Widsip*, which is dated sometime in the seventh century, is the earliest English writing we possess. There no doubt were other works, and of course a flourishing oral language, in what is now modern England, long before that. It is convenient, therefore, to give the date 450, a time when Teutonic adventurers, having initiated what was over the course of several centuries to become a major invasion, conquest, and settlement of Britain, had arrived in the island in sufficient numbers to found a linguistic community. We can call these people Anglo-Saxons and their language Old English. It is not as difficult to fix the end of the Old English period. The year of the last entry in *The Anglo-Saxon Chronicle*, 1154, closing out as it does a major literary document in the period, has become the traditional date to mark this event.

During this period of seven centuries the Anglo-Saxons evolved a language which sustained a major literature of the world. We can represent just a small portion of their production. Three texts, dated at about the year 1000, written in the Late West-Saxon dialect, the form of Old English used by King Alfred the Great (849–899), have been chosen. These are the texts:

1. *The Legend of St. Andrew. Anon.* The first forty-nine lines of this homiletic treatise—in this case a lively adventure designed to demonstrate the true wonder and glory of Christ as well as to teach the virtue of persever-

ance—constitute a representative passage of Old English prose. A complete glossary has been included.

2. *The Legend of St. Andrew.* The next thirty-two lines are given, with a literal inter-linear translation, to permit an observation of continuous development of a subject.

3. *The Assumption of St. John the Apostle.* Ælfric (955–1020). These first fifty lines represent the peak of Old English prose. They are followed by a partial glossary, some grammatical hints, and another translation.

THE LEGEND OF ST. ANDREW
lines 1–49, Ca. 975

Hēr segð þæt æfter þām þe Drihten Hǣlend Crīst tō
heofonum āstāh, þæt þā apostolī wǣron ætsomne; and
hīe sendon hlot him betwēonum, hwider hyra gehwylc
faran scolde tō lǣranne. Segþ þæt sē ēadiga Mathēus
gehlēat tō Marmadonia þǣre ceastre; segð þonne þæt þā   5
men þe on þǣre ceastre wǣron þæt hī hlāf ne ǣton, nē
wæter ne druncon, ac ǣton mana līchaman and heora
blōd druncon; and æghwylc man þe on þǣre ceastre cōm
ælþēodige, segð þæt hīe hine sōna genāmon and his ēagan
ūt āstungon, and hīe him sealdon āttor drincan þæt mid   10
myclum lybcræfte wæs geblanden, and mid þȳ þe hīe
þone drenc druncon, hraþe heora heorte wæs tōlēsed and
heora mōd onwended. Sē ēadiga Mathēus þā in ēode on
þā ceastre, and hraðe hīe hine genāmon and his ēagan
ūt āstungon, and hīe him sealdon āttor drincan, and hine   15
sendon on carcerne, and hīe hine hēton þæt āttor etan,
and hē hit etan nolde; for þon his heorte næs tōlēsed,
nē his mōd onwended; ac hē wæs simle tō Drihtne biddende mid myclum wōpe, and cwæð tō him, 'Mīn Drihten
Hǣlend Crīst, for þon wē ealle forlēton ūre cnēorisse,   20
and wǣron þē fylgende, and þū eart ūre ealra fultum, þā
þe on þē gelȳfaþ, beheald nū and geseoh hū þās men
þīnum þēowe dōð. And ic þē bidde, Drihten, þæt þū mē
forgife mīnra ēagna lēoht, þæt ic gesēo þā þe mē onginnað
dōn on þisse ceastre þā weorstan tintrego; and ne for-   25
lǣt mē, mīn Drihten Hǣlend Crīst, nē mē ne sele on
þone bitterestan dēaþ.'
   Mid þȳ þe hē þis gebed sē ēadiga Mathēus gecweden
hæfde, mycel lēoht and beorht onlēohte þæt carcern,
and Drihtnes stefn wæs geworden tō him on þǣm   30
lēohte cweþende, 'Mathēus, mīn sē lēofa, beheald on mē.'
Mathēus þā lōciende hē geseah Drihten Crīst, and
eft Drihtnes stefn wæs geworden tō him cweþende,
'Mathēus, wes þū gestrangod, and ne ondrǣd þū þē, for
þon ne forlǣte ic þē æfre, ac ic þē gefrēolsige of ealre   35
frēcennesse, and nālæs þæt ān, ac simle ealle þīne brō-
ðor, and ealle þā þe on mē gelȳfað on eallum tīdum oþ

Reprinted from *Bright's Anglo-Saxon Reader*, revised and enlarged, by J. R. Hulbert, by permission
of Holt, Rinehart and Winston, Inc.

ēcnesse. Ac onbīd hēr seofon and twēntig nihta, and
æfter þon ic sende tō þē Andrēas, þīnne brōþor, and hē
þē ūt ālǽdeþ of þissum carcerne, and ealle þā þe mid þē   *40*
syndon.' Mid þȳ þe þis gecweden wæs, Drihten him
eft tō cwæð, 'Sib sī mid þē, Mathēus.' Hē þā þurhwuniende mid gebedum wæs Drihtnes lof singende on þām
carcerne. And þā unrihtan men in ēodon on þæt carcern þæt hīe þā men ūt lǽdan woldon and him tō mete   *45*
dōn. Sē ēadiga Mathēus þā betȳnde his ēagan þȳ lǽs þā
cwelleras gesāwan þæt his ēagan geopenede wǽron; and
hīe cwǽdon him betwȳnum, 'Þrȳ dagas nū tō lāfe syndon
þæt wē hine willað ācwellan and ūs tō mete gedōn.'

ABBREVIATIONS USED

acc.–accusative
(adv.)–adverb
art.–article
comb.–in combination with
comp.–comparative
(conj.)–conjunction
dat.–dative
demons.–demonstrative
f.–feminine
gen.–genitive
ger.–gerund
imp.–imperative
ind.–indicative
inf.–infinitive
m.–masculine
n.–neuter
(n.)–noun
neg. part.–negative particle
nom.–nominative
(num.)–numeral

pers.–person
persl.–personal
pl.–plural
(poss. adj.)–possessive adjective
(poss. pron.)–possessive pronoun
p. ptc.–past participle
(prep.)–preposition
pres.–present
pret.–preterite
(pron.)–pronoun
(prop. n.)–proper noun
pr. ptc.–present participle
rel. part.–relative particle
sg.–singular
subj.–subjunctive
supl.-superlative
v.–vide
(v.)–verb
w.–with

GLOSSARY

The order is alphabetic, *æ* occurring between *ad* and *af*, and *ð* or *þ* occurring after *t*.

Each word in the text (with the line in the text where it occurs) is cited here, although in many instances an instruction will be given to look elsewhere. For example, the entry for ælþēodisc, in line 9, reads: **ælþēodisc,** v. *elþēodisc*. Under *elþēodisc* the definition of *ælþēodisc* will be found. Where several Modern English (MnE) equivalents for Old English (OE) words are cited, choose the word which makes for the most appropriate translation.

Since the object of this exercise is to enable you to construct a reliable comparison of OE syntax with MnE syntax, a certain amount of grammatical information is also cited with each word: part of speech, gender, case, and number, where applicable, and tense, person, number, and mood, where applicable. Some unusual constructions, or combinations of words, are also explained.

ac (*conj.*), but, unless: 7, 18, 35, 36, 38.

ācwellan (*v.*), kill: *inf.*, 49.

æfre (*adv.*), ever: 35.

æfter (*prep. w. dat., adv.*), after [a time or place]: *comb.*, æfter þām þe, at a time after, 1; æfter þon, after that time, 39.

æghwilc (*adj., pron.*), each, every: *nom. sg.*, 8.

æghwylc, *v.* æghwilc.

ælþēodisc, *v.* elþēodisc.

æton, *v.* etan.

ætsomne (*adv.*), together: 2.

ālædan (*v.*), lead, conduct: *3 sg. pres. ind.*, 40.

ālædeþ, *v.* alædan.

ān (*adj., num.*), one, a certain one, alone: *comb.* þæt ān, only that, 36.

and (*conj.*), and: 2, 7, etc. (total of 34 occurrences).

Andrēas (*prop. n.*), St. Andrew: 39.

apostol (*n.*), apostle: *m. nom. pl.*, 2.

apostoli, *v.* apostol.

āstāh, *v.* āstīgan.

āstīgan (*v.*), ascend, mount: *3 sg. pret. ind.*, 2.

āstingan (*v.*), pierce, pluck: *3 pl. pret. ind.*, 10, 15.

āstungon, *v.* āstingan.

āttor (*n.*), poison: *n. acc. sg.*, 10, 15, 16.

beheald, *v.* behealdan.

behealdan (*v.*), hold, guard, protect, behold, look: *imp. 2 sg.*, 22, 31.

bēon (*v.*), be: (eart: are) *2 sg. pres. ind.*, 21; (næs = ne + wæs: was not) *3 sg. pret. ind.*, 17; (sī: be) *2 sg. imp.*, 42; (syndon: are) *pl. pres. ind.*, 41, 48; (wæron: were) *pl. pret. ind.*, 2, 6, 21, 47; (wæs: was) *3 sg. pret. ind.*, 11, 12, 18, 30, 33, 41, 43; (wes: be) *2 sg. imp.*, 34.

beorht (*adj.*), bright, shining, glorious: *nom. sg.*, 29.

betwēonum (*prep. w. dat.*), among, between: 3, 48.

betwȳnum, *v.* betwēonum.

betȳnan (*v.*), close, finish, enclose, imprison: *3 sg. pret. ind.*, 46.

betȳnde, *v.* betȳnan.

biddan (*v.*), ask, entreat, request (*used w. acc. of pers. and gen. of things*): *1 sg. pres. ind.*, 23; *pr. ptc.*, 18.

bidde, *v.* biddan.

biddende, *v.* biddan.

biter (*adj.*), bitter, disastrous, fierce, severe: *supl. acc. sg.*, 27.

bitterestan, *v.* biter.

blōd (*n.*), blood: *n. acc. sg.*, 8.

brōþor (*n.*), brother: *m. acc. pl.*, 36; *m. acc. sg.*, 39.

carcern (*n.*), prison: *n. acc. sg.*, 29, 44; *n. dat. sg.*, 16, 40, 44.

carcerne, *v.* carcern.

ceaster (*n.*), city, fort, town: *f. dat. sg.*, 5, 6, 8, 25; *f. acc. sg.*, 14.

ceastre, *v.* ceaster.

cnēoriss (*n.*), family, generation, people, tribe: *f. acc. sg.*, 20.

cnēorisse, *v.* cnēoriss.

cōm, *v.* cuman.

Crist (*prop. n.*), Christ: *comb.* Drihten Hælend Crist, Lord Saviour Christ, 1, 20, 26; *comb.* Drihten Crist, Lord Christ, 32.

cuman (*v.*), come: *3 sg. pret. ind.*, 8.

cwǣdon, *v.* cweðan.

cwæð, *v.* cweðan.

cwelleras, *v.* cwellere.

cwellere (*n.*), executioner: *m. nom. pl.*, 47.

cweðan (*v.*), say, speak: *3 pl. pret. ind.*, 48; *3 sg. pret. ind.*, 19, 42; *pr. ptc.*, 31, 33.

cweþende, *v.* cweðan.

dæg (*n.*), day: *m. nom. pl.*, 48.

dagas, *v.* dæg.

dēaþ (*n.*), death; *m. acc. sg.*, 27.

dōn (*v.*), act, cause, do, place, put: *inf.*, 25, 46; *3 pl. pres. ind.*, 23.

dōð, *v.* dōn.

drenc (*n.*), drink: *m. acc. sg.*, 12.

drihten (*n.*), Lord, prince, ruler: *m. acc. sg.*, 23; *m. nom. sg.*, 41; *m. dat. sg.*, 18; *m. gen. sg.*, 30, 33, 43; *comb.* Crīst, Hǣlend, *v.* Crīst.
drihtne, *v.* drihten.
drihtnes, *v.* drihten.
drincan (*v.*), drink: *inf.*, 10. 15; *3 pl. pret. ind.*, 7, 8, 12.
druncon, *v.* drincan.

ēadig (*adj.*), blessed, happy, rich: *nom. sg.*, 4, 13, 28, 46.
ēadiga, *v.* ēadig.
ēagan, *v.* ēage.
ēage (*n.*), eye: *n. gen. pl.*, 24, 46, 47; *n. acc. pl.*, 9, 14.
ēagna, *v.* ēage.
eall (*adj.*), all; *nom. pl.*, 36, 37, 40; *gen. pl.*, 21, 35; *dat. pl.*, 37; (*adv.*), totally, completely: 20.
ealle, *v.* eall.
ealra, *v.* eall.
ealre, *v.* eall.
eallum, *v.* eall.
eart, *v.* bēon.
ēcnes (*n.*), eternity: *f. acc. sg.*, 38.
ēcnesse, *v.* ēcnes.
eft (*adv.*), again, afterwards, back: 33, 42.
elþēodisc (*adj.*), foreign, strange: *nom. sg.*, 9.
ēode, *v.* gān.
ēodon, *v.* gān.
etan (*v.*), eat: *inf.*, 16, 17; *3 pl. pret. ind.*, 6, 7.

faran (*v.*), go, march, travel: *inf.*, 4.
folgian (*v.*), follow, serve, obey: *pr. ptc.*, 21.
for (*prep. w. dat. & acc., conj.*), for, on account of: 20; *comb.* for þon, therefore, 17; *comb.* for þon, because, 34.
forgiefan (*v.*), give, grant, forgive: *2 sg. pres. subj.*, 24.
forgife, *v.* forgiefan.
forlǣt, *v.* forlǣtan.
forlǣtan (*v.*), leave, abandon, neglect: *1 sg. pres. ind.*, 35; *3 sg. pres. ind.*, 25; *3 pl. pret. ind.*, 20.

forlǣte, *v.* forlǣtan.
forlēton, *v.* forlǣtan.
frēcennes (*n.*), danger, harm: *f. dat. sg.*, 36.
frēcennesse, *v.* frēcennes.
fultum (*n.*), army, help: *m. nom. sg.*, 21.
fylgende, *v.* folgian.

gān (*v.*), go, walk, come: *3 sg. pret. ind.*, 13; *3 pl. pret. ind.*, 44.
gebed (*n.*), prayer: *n. acc. sg.*, 28; *n. dat. pl.*, 43.
gebedum, *v.* gebed.
geblandan (*v.*), blend, mix: *p. ptc.*, 11.
geblanden, *v.* geblandan.
gecweden, *v.* gecweðan.
gecweðan (*v.*), say, speak: *p. ptc.*, 28, 41.
gedōn (*v.*), do, cause to be, put into a certain condition: *inf.*, 49.
gefrēolsian (*v.*), deliver, set free: *1 sg. pres. ind.*, 35.
gefrēolsige, *v.* gefrēolsian.
gehlēat, *v.* gehlēotan.
gehlēotan (*v.*), cast or draw lots: *3 sg. pret. ind.*, 5.
gehwylc, gehwilc (*adj., pron.*), each, each one: 3.
gelīefan (*v.*), believe: *3 pl. pres. ind.*, 22, 37.
gelȳfað, *v.* gelīefan.
gelȳfaþ, *v.* gelīefan.
genāmon, *v.* geniman.
geniman (*v.*), take, seize; *3 pl. pret. ind.*, 9, 14.
geopenede, *v.* geopenian.
geopenian (*v.*), open: *pl. p. ptc.*, 47.
gesāwan, *v.* gesēon.
geseah, *v.* gesēon.
gesēo, *v.* gesēon.
geseoh, *v.* gesēon.
gesēon (*v.*), see, observe, consider: *3 pl. pret. ind.*, 47; *3 sg. pret. ind.*, 32; *1 sg. subj.*, 24; *2 sg. imp.*, 22.
gestrangian (*v.*), strengthen: *p. ptc.*, 34.
gestrangod, *v.* gestrangian.
geworden, *v.* geweorþan.
geweorþan (*v.*), happen, become, come to pass, make known: *p. ptc.*, 30, 33.

habban (*v.*), have: *3 sg. pret. ind.*, 29.

hæfde, *v.* habban.

Hǣlend (*n.*), Saviour: *v.* Crīst.

hātan (*v.*), command, order: *3 pl. pret. ind.*, 16.

hē, hēo, hit (*3 persl. pron.*), he, she, it: (hē: he), *m. nom. sg.*, 17, 18, 28, 32, 39, 42; (heora: their), *gen. pl.*, 7, 12, 13; (hī: they), *nom. pl.*, 6; (hīe: they), *nom. pl.*, 3, 9, 10, 11, 14, 15, 16, 45, 48; (him: to him), *m. dat. sg.*, 3, 10, 15, 19, 30, 33, 41, 45, 48; (hine: him), *m. acc. sg.*, 9, 14, 15, 16, 49; (his: his), *m. gen. sg.*, 9, 14, 17, 18, 46, 47; (hit: it), *m. acc. sg.*, 17; (hyra: their), *gen. pl.*, 3.

heofon (*n.*), heaven: *m. dat. pl.*, 2.

heofonum, *v.* heofon.

heora, *v.* hē.

heorte (*n.*), heart: *f. gen. pl.*, 12; *f. gen. sg.*, 17.

hēr (*adv.*), here: 1, 38.

hēton, *v.* hātan.

hi, *v.* hē.

hie, *v.* hē.

him, *v.* hē.

hine, *v.* hē.

his, *v.* hē.

hit, *v.* hē.

hlāf (*n.*), bread, loaf: *m. acc. sg.*, 6.

hlot (*n.*), lot: *n. acc. sg.*, 3; *comb.* sendon hlot, cast lots, 3.

hraðe, *v.* hraþe.

hraþe (*adv.*), quickly, soon: 12, 14.

hū (*adv.*), how: 22.

hwider (*adv.*), whither, to what place: 3.

hyra, *v.* hē.

ic (*1st persl. pron.*), I: (ic: I), *nom. sg.*, 23, 24, 35, 39; (mē: to or on me), *dat. sg.*, 23, 24, 31, 37; (mē: me), *acc. sg.*, 26; (mīn: my), *gen. sg.*, 19, 26, 31; (ūre: our), *gen. pl.*, 20, 21; (ūs: to or for us), *dat. pl.*, 49; (wē: we), *nom. pl.*, 20, 49.

in (*prep. w. dat. & acc.*), in, into: 13, 44.

lǣdan (*v.*), bring, conduct, lead: *inf.*, 45.

lǣran (*v.*), teach, advise: *ger.* (tō lǣranne), 4.

lǣs (*comp. adv.*), less: *comb.* þy lǣs (*conj.*), lest, 46.

lāf (*n.*), remainder: *f. dat. sg. comb.* tō lāfe, remaining, 48.

lāfe, *v.* lāf.

lēof (*adj.*), beloved, dear: *nom. sg.*, 31.

lēofa, *v.* lēof.

lēoht (*n.*), brightness, light: *n. acc. sg.*, 24; *n. nom. sg.*, 29; *n. dat. sg.*, 31.

lēohte, *v.* leoht.

lichaman, *v.* līchoma.

lichoma (*n.*), body: *m. gen. sg.*, 7.

lōcian (*v.*), look: *pres. ptc.*, 32.

lōciende, *v.* lōcian.

lof (*n.*), praise, glory, song of praise: *m. acc. sg.*, 43.

lybcræft (*n.*), skillful use of drugs or poison: *m. dat. sg.*, 11.

lybcræfte, *v.* lybcræft.

mon, *v.* monn.

manna, *v.* monn.

Marmadonia (*prop. n.*), said to be a city among the anthropophagi: 5.

Mathēus (*prop. n.*), St. Matthew: 4, 13, 28, 31, 32, 34, 42, 46.

mē, *v.* ic.

men, *v.* monn.

mete (*n.*), meat, food: *m. dat. sg.*, 45, 49.

micel (*adj.*), much, great, large: *nom. sg.*, 29; *dat. sing.*, 11, 19.

mid (*prep. w. dat. & acc.*), with: 10, 19, 40, 42, 43; *comb.* mid þȳ þe, when, 11, 28, 41.

min, *v.* ic.

minra (*poss. adj.*), my, mine; *gen. pl.*, 24.

mōd (*n.*), mind, mood, courage: *n. nom. sg.*, 13, 18.

monn (*n.*), man: *m. nom. sg.*, 8; *m. gen. pl.*, 7; *m. nom. pl.*, 6, 22, 44; *m. acc. pl.*, 45.

mycel, *v.* micel.

myclum, *v.* micel.

næs, *v.* bēon.

nālæs (*adv.*), not at all: 36.

ne (*neg. part.*), not: 6, 7, 25, 26, 34, 35.

nē (*adj., conj.*), and not, nor: 6, 18, 26.

niht (*n.*), night: *f. gen. pl.*, 38. (Literally 'of nights;' i.e., a number of days.)

nihta, *v.* niht.

nolde, *v.* willan.

nū (*adv.*), now: 22, 48.

of (*prep. w. dat.*), of, from, concerning, among: 35, 40.

on (*prep. w. dat. & acc.*), on, at, in, during, into, among, against: 6, 8, 13, 16, 22, 25, 26, 30, 31, 37, 43, 44.

onbid, *v.* onbīdan.

onbidan (*v.*), abide, wait, tarry: *2 sg. imp.*, 38.

ondrǣd, *v.* ondrǣdan.

ondrǣdan (*v.*), fear: *2 sg. imp.*, 34.

onginnan (*v.*), begin, attempt: *3 pl. pres. ind.*, 24.

onginnað, *v.* onginnan.

onlēohte, *v.* onlȳhtan.

onlȳhtan (*v.*), enlighten, illuminate: *3 sg. pret. ind.*, 29.

onwendan (*v.*), turn, change, overturn, amend: *p. ptc.*, 13, 18.

onwended, *v.* onwendan.

oþ (*prep. w. acc.*), up to, as far as, until: 37.

scolde, *v.* sculan.

sculan (*v.*), shall, ought, be necessary: *3 sg. pret. ind.*, 4.

sē (*art. & demons. pron.*), the, that: (sē: the, that), *m. nom. sg.*, 4, 13, 28, 31, 46; (þā: the, that, those), *f. acc. sg.*, 14; *nom. pl.*, 2, 5, 21, 24, 37, 46, 48; *acc. pl.*, 25, 45; (*comb.* þā þe, *v.* þe.); (þām: the, that, those), *n. dat. sg.*, 43; (þǣm: the, that, those), *n. dat. sg.*, 30; (þǣre: the, that), *f. dat. sg.*, 5, 6, 8; (þæt: the, that), *n. acc. sg.*, 16, 29, 44; (*comb.* þæt an, *v.* an); (þon: whom), *rel. pron.*, 20; (þon, *comb.* æfter þon, *v.* æfter); (þone: the, that), *m. acc. sg.*, 12, 27.

sealdon, *v.* sellan.

secgan (*v.*), say, tell: *3 sg., pres. ind.*, 1, 4, 5, 9.

segð, *v.* secgan.

segþ, *v.* secgan.

sele, *v.* sellan.

sellan (*v.*), give, sell: *2 sg. pres. ind.*, 26; *3 pl. pret. ind.*, 10, 15.

sendan (*v.*), send: *1 sg. pres. ind.*, 39; *3 pl. pret. ind.*, 16; sendon hlot, 3, *v.* hlot.

sende, *v.* sendan.

sendon, *v.* sendan.

seofon (*num.*), seven: 38

sī, *v.* bēon.

sib (*n.*), friendship, peace: *f. nom. sg.*, 42.

simle, *v.* symble.

singan (*v.*), sing, compose poetry: *pres. ptc.*, 43.

singende, *v.* singan.

sona (*adv.*), at once, immediately: 9.

stefn (*n.*), voice, sound: *f. nom. sg.*, 30, 33.

symble (*adv.*), ever, always: 18, 36.

syndon, *v.* bēon.

tid (*n.*), time, hour, tide: *f. dat. pl.*, 37.

tidum, *v.* tīd.

tintreg (*n.*), torment, torture: *n. acc. pl.*, 25.

tintrego, *v.* tintreg.

tō (*prep. w. dat.*), to, at, for: 1, 5, 18, 19, 30, 33, 39, 42, 45, 49; tō lāfe, *v.* lāf; *signal of gerund,* tō lǣranne, *v.* lǣran.

tōlēsed, *v.* tōlȳsan.

tōlȳsan (*v.*), unhinge, loosen, relax: *p. ptc.*, 12, 17.

twēntig (*num.*), twenty: 38.

þā (*adv., conj.*), then, when: 13, 32, 42, 44, 46.

þā, *v.* sē.

þǣm, *v.* sē.

þǣre, *v.* sē.

þæt (*conj.*), that, so that: 1, 2, 4, 5, 6, 9, 10, 23, 24, 45, 47, 49; *comb.* þæt ān, *v.* ān.

þæt, *v.* sē.

þām, *comb.* after þām þe, *v.* æfter.

þām, *v.* sē.

þās, *v.* þēs.

þe (*rel. part.*), who: 6, 8, 22, 24, 37, 40; *comb.* æfter þām þe, *v.* æfter; *comb.* mid þȳ þe, *v.* mid; *comb.* þā þe, those: 37.

þē, *v.* þū.

þēow (*n.*), servant: *m. dat. sg.*, 23.

þēowe, v. þēow.

þēs (demons. pron.), this: (þās: these), nom. pl., 22; (þis: this), n. acc. sg., 28; n. nom. sg., 41; (þisse: this), f. dat. sg., 25; (þissum: this), m. dat. sg., 40.

þin (poss. pron.), thine, your: þīne, acc. pl., 36; þīnne, acc. sg., 39; þīnum, dat. sg., 23.

þon, v. æfter, for, sē; comb. for þon, because, 34; comb. for þon, therefore, 17.

þone, v. sē.

þonne (adv.), then: 5.

þri (num.), three: 48.

þrȳ, v. þrī.

þū (2 persl. pron.), you: (þū: you), nom. sg., 21, 23, 34; (þē: you, thee), acc. sg., 21, 23, 34, 35, 40; (þē: you, thee), dat. sg., 22, 39, 40, 42.

þurhwunian (v.), continue, be steadfast: pr. ptc., 42.

þurhwuniende, v. þurhwunian.

þȳ, v. lǣs, mid.

unriht (adj.), wicked, wrong: nom. pl., 44.

unrihtan, v. unriht.

ūre, v. ic.

ūs, v. ic.

ūt (adv.), out: 10, 15, 40, 45.

wǣron, v. bēon.

wæs, v. bēon.

wæter (n.), water: n. acc. sg., 7.

wē, v. ic.

weorstan, v. yfel.

wes, v. bēon.

willan (v.), will, wish, be about to: 1 pl. pres. ind., 49; 3 pl. pret. ind., 45; nolde (comb. ne plus willan), 3 sg. pret. ind., 17.

willað, v. willan.

woldon, v. willan.

wōp (n.), weeping, lamentation: m. dat. sg., 19.

wōpe, v. wōp.

yfel (adj.), evil, bad: supl. acc. pl. (weorstan), 25.

QUESTIONS

The first thing you might notice about the text is that a good many of the letters have a dash printed above them; e.g., þām and tō, in line 1. It is a macron, a diacritical mark over a vowel or diphthong to indicate that it is 'long.' At this time ignore it; it will be of use when you turn to the exercise on phonology. Modern editions of Old English texts contain this marking; it is not used in editions of Middle English or Early Modern English texts.

1. Translate the passage into Modern English. First make a literal, word-for-word rendering; then transcribe into your normal composition. At first glance this might seem a formidable task, but by using the glossary wisely you will find it less frightening. The first two lines are worked out in this manner:

a. List all the words | b. List grammatical information and equivalents
--- | --- | ---
hēr | adv. | here
segð | 3 sg. pres. ind. | says, tells
þæt | conj. or v. sē | that or the, that
after þām þe | adverbial | at a time after
Drihten Hælend Crīst | prop. n. | Lord Saviour Christ

tō	prep. or signal for ger.	to, at, for (or ger.)
heofonum	n., masc. dat. pl.	heavens
āstāh	3 sg. pret. ind.	ascended, mounted
þæt	conj. or v. sē	that or the, that
þā	adv., conj. or v. sē	then, when, or the
apostolī	n., masc. nom. pl.	apostles
wǣron	pl. pret. ind, bēon	were
ætsomne	adv.	together

c. Construct the first string—same word order as original—here (says, tells) (that, the) at a time after Lord Saviour Christ (to, at, for) heavens (ascended, mounted) (that, the) (then, when, the) apostles were together

d. Find each verb and its subject; we know the nominative case is the case for the subject
says, tells—?
ascended, mounted—Lord Saviour Christ
were—apostles

e. Eliminate, making use of your sense of context, what appear to be unlikely lexical choices
says—tells: either will do, choose one
that—the: 'the' cannot precede 'at a time after'; retain *that*
to—at—for: which fits best with the next verb? probably *to*
ascended—mounted: either will do, but *ascended* feels better
that—the: consider the next group; 'the' cannot precede 'any'; retain *that*
then—when—the: all can precede 'apostles,' but if 'when' or 'then' is selected, we should expect something to occur after 'together'; retain *the*

f. Construct the second string
here says that at a time after Lord Saviour Christ to heavens ascended that the apostles were together

g. We have not yet found a subject for 'says'; *here* cannot be the subject; supply *it*; such a construction is not unusual in OE

h. Articles do not always occur in OE where, in a similar MnE construction, we expect them to occur. Is there a noun here without an article where we would expect it? We would insert *the* before *heavens*. (Note: if it were 'heaven,' i.e., singular, MnE would not require an article; but it is plural, *heavens,* and therefore the article is required.) We may or may not choose to insert an article before *Lord Saviour Christ*. These, too, are not unusual constructions in OE

i. Construct the third string
here it says that at a time after the Lord Saviour Christ to the heavens ascended that the apostles were together

j. Rearrange the word order where you think MnE usage would suggest reordering and insert punctuation
It says here that at a time after the Lord Saviour Christ ascended to the heavens, that the apostles were together;

k. Do not worry about the antecedent of *it*. The translation is correct. The writer apparently is following the habit set by many writers of chronicles, who often begin with "It says here" or something like this: *Hēr gefeaht Ecgbryht cyning,* In this year (here) King Ecgbryht fought. The *it* may refer to some other document, real or imagined, or the writer may, as we have said, just be falling back on the habit of chroniclers

There is no real need to set down the results of your work in this eleven step format. The format is a representation of what actually must be done in order to translate the passage. You must consult the glossary, you must observe the grammatical information given there, and you must arrive at an accurate MnE rendering of the original text. Whatever short cuts you find, take them. Translate the rest of the passage. (Do not be discouraged if it takes you a few hours to do it. It is not unwise, either, for several persons to work together, so long as it is understood that each comes away from such an exercise with a comprehension, and some knowledge, of OE directly proportionate to the effort he expended. This next remark has nothing whatsoever to do with either this exercise or anything you do with this book; it is simply a corollary pronouncement. Nobody can *teach* anybody a second language, or how to read a second language: teachers can set out models and guides, but anyone who wishes to *learn* to *use* a second language has to *learn* it himself.)

2. Make a list showing each verb with its subject. Supply *hit* for *segð*. What does the verb inflectional ending *-on* signify? What does the verb inflectional ending *-an* signify? What do you make of the form *gesawan* in 1. 47? How do you explain it? Consult the glossary where necessary.

3. The personal endings for strong and weak verbs in the present and preterite indicative are shown in the following list:

Strong (and Weak, Class I)   *Weak, Class II*

Pres. Ind.

Sg. 1	-e	-ie
Sg. 2	-est	-ast
Sg. 3	-eþ	-aþ
Pl. 1, 2, 3	-aþ	-iaþ

Pret. Ind.

Sg. 1	-	-e
Sg. 2	-e	-est
Sg. 3	-	-e
Pl. 1, 2, 3	-on	-on

Find as many examples from the text to match the slots in this paradigm. Which slots are vacant? Do you find any occurrences of verbs which you cannot fit in any slot? What is the construction of *forgife* in 1. 24? What conclusion does this occurrence suggest? Consult the glossary where necessary.

4. Compare the constructions observed in questions 2 and 3 with their corresponding forms in MnE: write out several complete conjugations of MnE verbs, fitting the paradigm used in question 3. What differences do you observe between

the MnE and the OE paradigms? What can you conclude about the development of these verb forms from the OE period to the MnE period?

5. Set out all the forms of *bēon* which occur in the text in paradigmatic form and place their MnE equivalent forms next to them. What has been the development of 'be'? Would you say 'be' has been more or less stable than the strong and weak verbs?

6. Make a list of all verbal negation and interrogatory constructions and compare each with its MnE construction. What differences do you observe? Formulate a general statement about the function of the MnE 'carrier' (or auxilliary) 'do' in negative and interrogatory constructions. Would you say English has become more or less efficient in this regard?

7. The concept of substitution of linguistic forms is easily demonstrated by the occurrence of pronouns in MnE. For example, a) 'When John fell *he* hurt his knee' and b) 'When John fell *John* hurt his knee' have equivalent meaning. We can also say that pro-*verbs* occur in MnE; for example, a) 'I often run and so does John' and b) 'I often run and so does John run' have equivalent meaning, c) 'I don't run but John does' and d) 'I don't run but John runs' have equivalent meaning, and e) 'I have never run but John has' and f) 'I have never run but John has run' have equivalent meaning. These are occurrences of pro-verbs. Are there any occurrences of the pro-verb in OE?

8. Which nouns occur with articles? which without? Compare those occurrences with MnE practise.

9. Observe the occurrence of adjectives and adverbs. Are the modification patterns (the position of the modifier with respect to the word or element modified) similar or dissimilar to corresponding MnE practise?

10. How are relative patterns constructed in OE? Do you find any occurrence here of the practise in MnE of omitting the relative marker? (E.g., 'This is the man I saw' is equivalent in meaning to 'This is the man *whom* I saw.')

11. In the original text the word *and* occurs 34 times. In an accurate MnE translation of the passage, what might be the minimum occurrence of 'and'? What does this suggest about OE syntax?

12. In Exercise 14, "Phonological Change," you will see the text of "The Legend of St. Andrew" again. There the text is 'normalized,' i.e., the editor put the text into the form of Late West Saxon used by Alfred. Compare the two texts. What differences in spelling occur? What do those differences suggest? (What is a dialect? How may one dialect differ from another? If you were an editor, would you choose to normalize a text? Why?)

13. Consult your 'final' translation of this passage and compare it with the original text. If this were the only sample of OE you could examine, if there were no other data to consult, what would you say constitutes the most significant differences between OE and MnE? (There is a suggestion here, of course, for an essay or a class discussion—only to be followed at great risk, however, before the first twelve questions are answered.)

THE LEGEND OF ST. ANDREW

lines 50–96

Se eadiga Matheus þa gefelde xx daga. Þa Drihten Hælend Crist
the blessed Matthew then filled twenty days then Lord Savior Christ

cwæð to Andrea his apostole, mid þi þe he wæs in Achaia þam lande and
said to Andrew his apostle when he was in Achaia the land and

þær lærde his discipuli, he cwæð, 'Gang on Marmadonia ceastre, and alæd
there taught his disciples he said go to Marmadonia city and lead

þanon Matheum þinne broþor of þæm carcerne, for þon þe nu git þry
thence Matthew your brother from the prison because now still three

dagas to lafe syndon, þæt hie hine willað acwellan and him to mete
days remaining are that they him will kill and him to meat 5

gedon.' Se haliga Andreas him andswarode, and he cwæð, 'Min Drihten
do the holy Andrew him answered and he said my Lord

Hælend Crist, hu mæg ic hit on þrim dagum gefaran? Ac ma wen is
Savior Christ how might I it in three days travel but better hope is

þæt þu onsende þinne engel se hit mæg hrædlicor gefaran, for þon,
that you will send your angel who it might more readily travel because

min Drihten, þu wast þæt ic eam flæsclic man, and ic hit ne mæg hrædlice
my Lord you know that I am fleshly man and I it not might readily

gefaran, for þon þe, min Drihten, se siðfæt is þider to lang, and ic
travel because my Lord the journey is thither too long and I 10

þone weg ne can.' Drihten him to cwæð, 'Andreas, geher me for þon þe ic þe
the way not know Lord him to said Andrew hear me because I you

geworhte, and ic þinne sið gestaþelode and getrymede. Gang nu to þæs sæs
made and I your journey established and prepared go now to the sea's

waroðe mid þinum discipulum, and þu þær gemetest scip on þam waroðe;
shore with your disciples and you there will meet ship on the shore

and astig on þæt mid þinum discipulum.' And mid þy þe he þis cwæð,
and mount on that with your disciples and when he this said

Drihten Hælend ða git wæs sprecende and cwæð, 'Sib mid þe and mid
Lord Savior then still was speaking and said peace [be] with you and 15

Reprinted from *Bright's Anglo-Saxon Reader*, revised and enlarged by J. R. Hulbert, by permission of Holt, Rinehart and Winston, Inc.

eallum þinum discipulum.' And he astag   on   heofonas.
with   all your disciples   and he ascended to [the] heavens

Se haliga Andreas þa   aras on mergen, and he eode to þære sæ mid
the holy   Andrew then arose next morning and he went to the   sea with

his discipulum, and he geseah scip on þam waroðe and þry   weras on þam
his disciples   and he saw   ship on the   shore   and three men   in it

sittende; and he wæs gefeonde mid mycle gefean, and him to cwæð, 'Broðor,
sitting   and he was rejoicing with great delight and them to said   brothers

hwider wille ge   faran mid þis medmiclum scipe?' Drihten Hælend wæs
whither will you   travel with this small   ship   Lord   Savior   was   *20*

on þam scipe swa se   steorreðra, and his twegen englas mid him, þa
on the ship as the helmsman   and his two   angels with him who

wæron gehwyrfede   on manna onsyne. Drihten Crist him þa   to cwæð, 'On
were   transformed in men's shape Lord   Christ him then to said   to

Marmadonia ceastre.' Se haliga Andreas him andswarode, and he cwæð,
Marmadonia city   the holy   Andrew him answered   and he said

'Broðor, onfoh us mid eow on þæt scip and gelædað us on þa ceastre.'
brothers take   us with you in that ship and lead   us to the city

Drihten him to cwæð, 'Ealle men fleoð of   þære ceastre; to hwæm wille
Lord   him to said   all   men flee from the city   why   will   *25*

ge   þider   faran?' Se haliga Andreas him andswarode, he cwæð, 'Medmycel
you thither travel   the holy   Andrew him answered   he said   small

ærende we þider habbað, and us   is þearf þæt we hit þeh   gefyllon.'
errand we thither have   and [to] us is need that we it nonetheless fullfil

Drihten Hælend him to cwæð, 'Astigað on þis scip to us, and sellað us
Lord   Savior him to said   mount   in this ship with us and give   us

eowerne færsceat.' Se haliga Andreas him andswarode, 'Gehyrað
your   fare   the holy   Andrew him answered   hear

gebroðor, nabbað we færsceat, ac we syndon discupli Drihtnes Hælendes
brother   not have we fare   but we are   disciples [of] Lord Savior   *30*

Cristes, þa   he geceas; and þis bebod   he us sealde, and he cwæð, "þonne
Christ   whom he chose and this command he us gave   and he said   when

ge   faran godspel to lærenne, þonne   nabbe ge   mid eow hlaf ne feoh,   ne
you travel gospel teaching   then not have you with you bread nor property nor

twifeald hrægl." Gif þu þonne wille mildheortnesse mid us don, saga us
twofold garments if you then will gentleness   with us do   tell us

þæt hrædlice; gif þu þonne nelle, gecyð   us swa þeah þone weg.' Drihten
that quickly   if you then no   will show us nonetheless the way   Lord

Hælend him to cwæð, 'Gif þis gebod   eow   wære geseald fram eowrum
Savior   them to said   if   this command [to] you were   given   by   our   *35*

Drihtene, astigað hider mid gefean on min scip.'
Lord   climb   hither with joy   in my   ship

QUESTIONS

You will notice that in this selection the macron has not been printed to mark the length of vowels and diphthongs.

1. Rewrite the interlinear translation in your normal composition style.
2. We may use this passage to illustrate how the grammatical devices of OE differ from the grammatical devices of MnE. A grammatical device is a structural signal inherent in the system of a language which is employed (in oral as well as written communication) by users of the language to indicate relationships which exist between various elements of the language. Syntax is, from this point of view, the study and perception of the grammatical signals, or devices, which a language employs. OE relied heavily on inflection to provide signals of grammatical, or structural meaning. Lexical (referential), or 'dictionary,' meaning of words does not indicate these relationships: structural (differential), or grammatical, meaning is signaled by various devices. In 1. 5, for example, we read *hie hine willað acwellan.* Because we know that *hie* is nom. pl. (and accords with the -að of the verb) and that *hine* is acc. sg., we know which is the subject and which is the object, and we know therefore that we must read 'they will kill him.' *Inflections,* then, are a signal. To an extent larger than we often realize, they are also a signal in MnE. For example, 'they' and 'him' in MnE are distinguished by their form. But observe, too, that we cannot say ' *they him will kill,' because in this pattern we expect the verb to precede its object, and we therefore say 'they will kill him,' even though, it might be argued, the formal difference between 'they' and 'him' should be a sufficient signal to make sure that we know which is subject and which is object. In this case, as in so many others (fortunately for ease of communication), MnE shows its tendency to display redundant signals. Thus the pattern itself, *word order,* is a grammatical signal. The occurrence, in 1. 12, of *sæs waroðe* (sea's shore), and, in 1. 20, of *manna onsyne* (the shape of men), suggests that the genitive case (and the function that it performs) in OE, signalled by inflection, may, in MnE, be signalled by either word order or by the use of a *function word,* 'of.' In OE the genitive relationship desired between 'sea' and 'shore' could be signaled only by inflection, but in MnE we may signal that same relationship by making use of all three devices:
inflection—sea's shore
word order—sea shore ('shore sea' is not equivalent)
function word—shore of the sea
The very existence of these three devices—inflection, word order, and function word —constitutes an excellent base for a comparison of OE syntax with MnE syntax. (Two other signals familiar to speakers of MnE—*derivational contrast* and *intonation contour*—the differences, that is, between *good* and *goodness,* where *-ness* signals a noun, and between the two occurrences of *suspect* in 'we suspéct the súspect,' that sort of thing, are not taken up in this exercise.)

Examine this passage, and those of Exercises 1 and 3, to determine where MnE usage, in the same compositional situation, would (1) *require* a different signalling system from what you find in the original and (2) where it would *permit* a different signalling system. To make use of contemporary syntactical terms, make a comparison (and write a report setting out your conclusions) of the *obligatory* and *optional* constructions available in OE and MnE composition.

3. Would you say, having completed that study, that the grammar of English has been 'simplified' during the years which separate us from the OE period? Consult Sidney's *Apology for Poetry,* published in 1595, especially where he writes that English 'wanteth (i.e., lacks) grammar.' What do you suppose he might have meant? Was he right?

(Having got you through the first 96 lines of this text—as it is printed in *Bright's Anglo-Saxon Reader*—it is only fair to point out to some of you, who might want to learn what happened to Andrew in Marmadonia—and things get rather interesting for Matthew and Andrew—that you can find translations of the rest of the story; but, give it a thought, some of you could now read the whole text in Old English, and the text is contained in many of the Old English anthologies.)

THE ASSUMPTION OF ST. JOHN THE APOSTLE
Ælfric, ca. 990, lines 1–52

Iōhannes sē godspellere, Crīstes dȳrling, wearð on ðysum
dæge tō heofenan rīces myrhðe þurh Godes nēosunge ge-
numen. Hē wæs Crīstes mōddrian sunu, and hē hine lufode
synderlīce, nā swā micclum for ðǣre mǣglican sibbe swā for
ðǣre clǣnnysse his ansundan mægðhādes. Hē wæs on mægð-   5
hāde Gode gecoren, and hē on ēcnysse on ungewemmedum
mægðhāde þurhwunode. Hit is gerǣd on gewyrdelicum
racum þæt hē wolde wīfian, and Crīst wearð tō his gyftum
gelaðod. Þā gelamp hit þæt æt ðām gyftum wīn wearð
āteorod. Sē Hǣlend ðā hēt þā ðēningmen āfyllan six   *10*
stǣnene fatu mid hlūttrum wætere, and hē mid his bletsunge
þæt wæter tō æðelum wīne āwende. Þis is þæt forme tācn
ðe hē on his menniscnysse openlīce geworhte. Þā wearð
Iōhannes swā onbryrd þurh þæt tācn, þæt hē ðærrihte his
brȳde on mægðhāde forlēt, and symle syððan Drihtne   *15*
folgode, and wearð ðā him inweardlīce gelufod, for ðan ðe
hē hine ætbrǣd þām flǣsclicum lustum. Witodlīce ðisum
lēofan leorningcnihte befæste sē Hǣlend his mōdor, þā þū hē
on rōdehengene manncynn ālȳsde, þæt his clǣne līf ðæs
clǣnan mǣdenes Marīan gȳmde; and hēo ðā on hyre   *20*
swyster suna þēnungum wunode.
    Eft on fyrste, æfter Crīstes ūpstige tō heofonum, rīxode
sum wælhrēow cāsere on Rōmāna rīce, æfter Nerōne, sē
wæs Domiciānus gehāten, crīstenra manna ēhtere: sē hēt
āfyllan āne cȳfe mid weallendum ele, and þone mǣran   *25*
godspellere þǣron hēt bescūfan; ac hē ðurh Godes gescyldnysse ungewemmed of ðām hātum bæðe ēode. Eft, ðā ðā
sē wælhrēowa ne mihte ðæs ēadigan apostoles bodunge
ālecgan, þā āsende hē hine on wræcsīð tō ānum īgeoðe þe
is Paðmas gecīged, þæt hē ðǣr þurh hungres scearpnysse   *30*
ācwǣle. Ac sē ælmihtiga Hǣlend ne forlēt tō gȳmelēaste
his gelufedan apostol, ac geswutelode him on ðām wræcsīðe
þā tōweardan onwrigennysse, be ðǣre hē āwrāt ðā bōc ðe is
gehāten 'Apocalipsis': and sē wælhrēowa Domiciānus on
ðām ylcan gēare wearð ācweald æt his witena handum;   *35*
and hī ealle ānmōdlīce rǣddon þæt ealle his gesetnyssa
āȳdlode wǣron. Þā wearð Nerua, swīðe ārfæst man, tō
cāsere gecoren. Be his geþafunge gecyrde sē apostol

Reprinted from Sweet's *Anglo-Saxon Reader*, revised by C. T. Onions, 14th ed. (Oxford: The Clarendon Press, 1959), by permission of The Clarendon Press, Oxford.

ongēan mid micclum wurðmynte, sē ðe mid hospe tō
wræcsīðe āsend wæs. Him urnon ongēan weras and wīf   *40*
fægnigende and cweðende: 'Gebletsod is sē ðe cōm on
Godes naman.'

Mid þām ðe sē apostol Iōhannes stōp intō ðære byrig
Ephesum, þā bær man him tōgēanes ānre wydewan līc
tō byrigenne; hire nama wæs Drūsiāna. Hēo wæs swīðe   *45*
gelȳfed and ælmesgeorn, and þā ðearfan, ðe hēo mid cystigum mōde eallunga āfēdde, drēorige mid wōpe ðām līce
folgodon. Þā hēt sē apostol ðā bære settan, and cwæð: 'Mīn
Drihten, Hælend Crīst, ārǣre ðē, Drūsiāna; ārīs, and gecyrr
hām, and gearca ūs gereordunge on þīnum hūse.' Drūsiāna   *50*
þā ārās swilce of slǣpe āwreht, and carfull be ðæs apostoles
hǣse hām gewende.

GLOSSARY

In this glossary words not found in the glossary for "The Legend of St. Andrew"
will be defined *in the order in which they occur,* cited by the line number from the
text. Since only the grammatical information not found in the first glossary is given
here, *both* glossaries may have to be consulted during the course of this exercise.
You should note, by examining the texts closely, that some letters are used inter-
changeably; e.g., 'i and y' and 'þ and ð' are frequently interchanged. It is
also expected that you will know, in line two, that 'Godes' is the genitive singular
of God, that, in line fifteen, 'forlēt' is certainly the same verb as 'forlǣtan' in the
first glossary, that sort of thing. In other words, you will have learned some OE
by the time you reach this exercise. And, of course, you also have the translations
to help you over rough spots.

1 **Iōhannes** (*prop. n.*), St. John;
godspellere (*n.*), evangelist: *m. nom.
sg.*;**dȳrling** (*n.*), favorite: *m. nom.
sg.*; **wearð,** *3 sg. pret. ind. of* weorþan,
become, be, made, happen, *fre-
quently used as passive auxilliary.*

2 **rices** (*n.*), kingdom: *n. gen. sg.*;
myrhðe (*n.*), mirth, joy: *f. dat. sg.*;
nēosunge (*n.*), visitation: *f. dat.
sg.*

3 **mōddrian** (*n.*), aunt: *f. gen. sg.*; **sunu**
(*n.*), son: *m. acc. sg.*

4 **synderlice** (*adv.*), especially; **mǣglican
sibbe:** relationship of kin.

5 **clǣnnysse** (*n.*), cleanness, purity,
chastity: *f. dat. sg.*; **ansundan** (*adj.*),
sound, uninjured; **mægðhādes** (*n.*),
virginity: *m. gen. sg.*

6 **gecoren,** *p. ptc. of* cēosan, choose;
ungewemmedum (*ptc. as adj.*), undefiled.

7 **gerǣd,** *p. ptc. of* rǣdan, read, advise,
discuss; **gewyrdelicum** (*adj.*),
historical: *dat. pl.*

8 **racum** (*n.*), narrative, account,
reckoning: *f. dat. pl.*; **wifian,** *inf.,* to
marry; **gyftum** (*n.*), dowry, *in pl.,*
marriage, wedding: *f. dat. pl.*

9 **gelaðod,** *p. ptc. of* laðian, invite,
summon; **gelamp,** *3 sg. pret. ind. of*
limpan, happen; **win** (*n.*), wine: *n.
nom. sg.*

10 **ātēorod,** *p. ptc. of* ātēorian, fail,
become exhausted; **ðēningmen** (*n.*),
servant: *m. acc. pl.*; **āfyllan,** *inf.,* to
fill; **six** (*num.*), six.

11 **stænene** (*cf.* stān: stone), of stone; **fatu** (*n.*), vessel, jar: *n. acc. pl.*; **hlūttrum** (*adj.*), clear: *dat. sg.*; **bletsunge** (*n.*), blessing: *f. gen. sg.*

12 **æðelum** (*adj.*), noble, excellent: *dat. sg.*; **āwende**, *3 sg. pret. ind.* of āwendan, turn, change; **forme** (*ordinal num.*), first; **tācn** (*n.*), sign, token, miracle; *n. nom. sg.*

13 **menniscnysse** (*n.*), incarnation: *f. dat. sg.*; **openlice** (*adv.*), publicly, openly; **geworhte**, *3 sg. pret. ind.* of gewyrcan, work, perform.

14 **onbryrd,** *p. ptc.* of onbryrdan, inspire, exhalt; **þærrihte** (*adv.*), forthwith, at once.

15 **brȳde** (*n.*), bride: *f. acc. sg.*; **syððan** (*adv., conj.*), since, after that, afterwards.

16 **inweardlice** (*adv.*), inwardly, deeply; **gelufod,** *p. ptc.* of lufian, love.

17 **ætbræd**, *3 sg. pret. ind.* of ætbregdan, take away, deprive, release; **flæsclicum** (*adj.*), fleshly, carnal: *dat. pl.*; **lustum** (*n.*), lust, desire, pleasure: *m. dat. pl.*; **witodlice** (*adv.*), truly, indeed.

18 **leorningcnihte** (*n.*), disciple, pupil: *m. dat. sg.*; **befæste**, *3 sg pret. ind.* of befæstan, fasten, fix, entrust, put in safe keeping; **mōdor** (*n.*), mother: *f. acc. sg.*

19 **rōdehengene** (*n.*), crucifixion: *f. dat. sg.*; **manncynn** (*n.*), mankind: *n. acc. sg.*; **ālȳsde**, *3 sg. pret. ind.* of ālȳsan, loosen, release, redeem, ransom; **clǣne** (*adj.*), clean, pure: *nom. sg.*; **lif** (*n.*), life: *n. nom. sg.*

20 **mædenes** (*n.*), maiden, virgin: *n. gen. sg.*; **Marian** (*prop. n.*), Mary; **gȳmde**, *3 sg. pret. subj.* of gīeman, care for, regard.

21 **swyster** (*n.*), sister: *f. gen. sg.*; **þenungum** (*n.*), service, ministration: *f. dat. pl.*; **wunode**, *3 sg. pret. ind.* of wunian, dwell, remain, live.

22 **eft on fyrste** (*adverbial*), later on; **upstige** (*n.*), ascension: *m. dat. sg.*;

rixode, *3 sg. pret. ind.* of rīcsian, rule, reign.

23 **sum** (*pron., adj.*), some, some one, certain, certain one: *nom. sg.*; **wælhrēow** (*adj.*), murderous, cruel: *nom. sg.*; **cāsere** (*n.*), emperor: *m. nom. sg.*; **Rōmāna** (*prop. n.*), Roman: *gen. pl.*; **Nerōne** (*prop. n.*), Nero.

24 **Domiciānus** (*prop. n.*), Domitian; **gehāten**, *p. ptc.* of gehatan, name; **cristenra** (*adj.*), Christian: *gen. pl.*; **ēhtere** (*n.*), persecutor: *m. nom. sg.*

25 **āfyllan**, *inf.*, to fill; **cȳfe** (*n.*), tub, vessel: *f. acc. sg.*; **weallendum**, *pres. ptc.* (*used as adj.*) of weallan, boil; **ele** (*n.*), oil: *m. dat. sg.*

26 **bescūfan**, *inf.*, to shove, thrust; **gescyldnysse** (*n.*), care, protection: *f. acc. sg.*

27 **ungewemmed** (*p. ptc. as adj.*), undefiled, pure, sound: *dat. pl.*; **hātum** (*adj.*), hot: *dat. sg.*; **bæðe** (*n.*), bath: *n. dat. sg.*

28 **mihte**, *3 sg. pret. subj.* of magan, may, be able; **bodunge** (*n.*), preaching: *f. acc. sg.*

29 **ālecgan**, *inf.*, to refute; **āsende**, *3 sg. pret. ind.* of āsendan, send; **wræcsið** (*n.*), exile: *m. dat. sg.*; **īgeoðe** (*n.*), small island: *m. dat. sg.*

30 **Paðmas** (*prop. n.*), Patmos: **geciged**, *p. ptc.* of gecīegan, call, name; **hungres** (*n.*), hunger: *m. gen. sg.*; **scearpnysse** (*n.*), sharpness: *f. acc. sg.*

31 **ælmihtiga** (*adj.*), almighty: *nom. sg.*; **gȳmelēaste** (*n.*), neglect: *f. dat. sg.*

32 **geswutelode**, *3 sg. pret. ind.* of geswutelian, show, make manifest.

33 **tōweardan** (*adj.*), future: *acc. sg.*; **onwrigennysse** (*n.*), revelation: *f. acc. sg.*; **be ðære** (*prep.*), on account of which; **āwrāt**, *3 sg. pret. ind.* of āwrītan, write, compose; **bōc** (*n.*), book: *f. acc. sg.*

35 **ylcan** (*pron.*), the same: *dat. sg.*; **gēare** (*n.*), year: *n. dat. sg.*; **witena** (*n.*), councilor: *m. gen. pl.*; **handum** (*n.*), hand: *f. dat. pl.*

36 ānmōdlice (*adv.*), unanimously; **rǣd-don**, *3 pl. pret. ind. of* rǣdan, advise, counsel; **gesetnyssa** (*n.*), decree: *f. acc. pl.*

37 **āȳdlode**, *pl. p. ptc. of* āȳdlian, annul; **Nerua** (*prop. n.*), Nerva; **swiðe** (*adv.*), very, exceedingly; **ārfæst** (*adj.*), honorable, virtuous, merciful: *nom. sg.*

38 **gecoren**, *p. ptc. of* gecēosan, choose, elect; **geþafunge** (*n.*), assent, permission: *f. dat. sg.*; **gecyrde**, *3 sg. pret. ind. of* geciernan, return.

39 **wurðmynte** (*n.*), honor, glory, reverence: *f. dat. sg.*; **hospe** (*n.*), contempt, insult: *m. dat. sg.*

40 **urnon**, *3 pl. pret. ind. of* yrnan, run; **weras** (*n.*), man: *m. nom. pl.*; **wif** (*n.*), woman, wife: *f. nom. pl.*

41 **fægnigende**, *pres. ptc. of* fægnian, rejoice; **gebletsod**, *p. ptc. of* geblētsian, bless.

42 **naman** (*n.*), name: *m. acc. sg.*

43 **stōp**, *3 sg. pret. ind. of* steppan, step, advance, go; **byrig** (*n.*), fort, borough, town, city: *f. dat. sg.*

44 **Ephesum**, (*prop. n.*), Ephesus, ancient city in Ionia, near present city of Selsuk; **bær**, *3 sg. pret. ind. of* beran, bear; **wydewan** (*n.*), widow: *f. gen. sg.*; **lic** (*n.*), corpse, body: *n. acc. sg.*

45 **tō byrigenne**, *ger. of* byrgan, bury; **Drūsiana** (*prop. n.*).

46 **gelȳfed**, *p. ptc. of* gelīefan, believe (filled with belief); **ælmesgeorn** (*adj.*), generous, liberal of alms; **ðearfan** (*n.*), poor man: *m. nom. pl.*; **cystigum** (*adj.*), virtuous, charitable: *d. sg.*

47 **āfēdde**, *3 sg. pret. ind. of* āfēdan, feed, sustain; **drēorige** (*adj.*), sad, dreary: *nom. pl.*

48 **settan**, *inf.*, to set, place.

49 **ārǣre**, *3 sg. pres. subj. of* ārǣran, raise, erect; **āris**, *2 sg. imp. of* ārīsan, arise.

50. **hām** (*n.*), home: *m. acc. sg.*; **gearca**, *2 sg. imp. of* gearcian, prepare; **gereordunge** (*n.*), refection, meal: *f. acc. sg.*; **hūse** (*n.*), house: *n. dat. sg.*

51 **swilce** (*adv., conj.*), in such manner, thus; **slǣpe** (*n.*), sleep: *m. dat. sg.*; **āwreht**, *p. ptc. of* āweccan, awake, arouse; **carfull** (*adj.*), careful: *dat. sg.*

52 **hǣse** (*n.*), behest, command: *f. dat. sg.*; **gewende**, *3 sg. pret. ind. of* gewendan, return, go.

A LITTLE MORE GRAMMAR

Some significant differences between OE and MnE, which will shed some light on the shape of OE syntax, can be illustrated rather quickly. Some account of them must be taken in our consideration of the development of the English Language. What is set out here, of course, is in no way intended as a complete description: on the contrary, the examples are to be taken as hints in arriving at decent translations and, as well, a better view of the course of our language.

Negation

1. The verb in OE is transformed to the negative by placing *ne* immediately before it; *ne bād ðæt sweord*; the sword did not bite. Sometimes, when the idea of negation is stressed, *nā* or *nō* may occur, instead of *ne*.

2. *Ne* contracts with a following word beginning with a vowel or *h* or *w nis*, from *ne is*; *næfde*, from *ne hæfde*; *nillan*, from *ne willan*; etc.

3. *Ne* occurring before other than a finite verb is a conjunction; *ne bān ne limu*; neither bones nor limbs; *ne singan ne sprecan*; neither (to) sing nor (to) say.

4. *Nā* and *nō* are used to negate words which are not finite verbs; *sēo wæs þǣre cwēne þēow ond nā cwēn*; she was the queens' servant and no (not a) queen.

5. The use of multiple negatives in a structure is not unusual and is not an indication of sub-standard usage, as it might be in MnE; *ond Apollonius nān ðing ne æt*; and Apollonius did not eat a thing (lit., and A. no thing not ate; cf. MnE sub-s., didn't eat nothing).

Prepositions

Here is a list of some important OE prepositions, with MnE equivalents, and the cases they govern.

æfter	dat.	after, along, according to
ǣr	dat.	before
æt	dat.	at, from, by
be	dat.	by, along, about
ēac	dat.	besides, in addition to
for	dat.	before (a place), in front of, because of
fram	dat.	from, by
geònd	acc.	throughout, during
in	acc., dat.	in, into
mid	acc., dat.	among, with, by means of
of	dat.	from, of
on	acc., dat.	in, into, on
ongean	acc., dat.	against, towards
oþ	acc., dat.	up to, until
tō	gen.	at, for, so
tō	dat.	to, towards, at, near
þurh	acc., dat.	through, throughout, by means of
wiþ	acc., dat., gen.	against, opposite, alongside of, by, towards, upon, in the presence of, from, with

The OE *wiþ* suggests the necessity of relating all these words to the context in which they occur; e.g., *hū gefeul Ecgbryht cyning wiþ fīf and twēntig sciphlæsta æt Carrum*; what did King Ecgbryht do? Did he fight at Carhampton with twenty-five shiploads of men [i.e., on their side], or did he fight against them?

When it is said that prepositions 'govern a case' it is meant that the preposition determines the case of the noun, in most instances appearing after the preposition, with which (syntactically) it is associated: *tō mīn hūses*; at (for) my house: gen.; *fār tō þam lande*; travel to (towards, at, near) the land: dat.

Agreement

The grammatical property of concord (agreement) is observed in OE, as it is for all inflected languages. In MnE we must observe the property of agreement between subjects and verbs; 'he runs—they run.' We say the subject and verb must agree in number (sg. or pl.) and person (1, 2, 3). OE observes the same rule. But in addition, in OE (1) nouns, pronouns, and their modifiers must agree in number, gender, and case and (2) pronouns and their antecedents must agree in number and gender. While MnE displays some of this agreement (e.g., 'thirty white horses'; 'each of his wishes is granted'), the situation in OE is further complicated by the requirement for agreement in gender, where, not infrequently, a conflict exists between grammatical gender and natural gender.

MnE has dispensed (largely) with grammatical gender. The tendency is to relate gender with sex, and thus, for animate objects, to assign male, female, or common gender on natural grounds, and for inanimate objects, to assign neuter gender (no sex implied) universally. But in no instance does MnE, except in the case of personal pronouns, display any formal characteristic to signal gender. Occasionally, to be sure, we might speak of a sports car, or a boat, say, as 'she' or 'her,' but that is exceptional. In OE, however, objects were assigned an arbitrary gender, and the structure of the language provides formal characteristics (inflectional endings) to signal gender. Thus, for example, *sunne*; sun: f.; *mōna*; moon: m.; *ēage*; eye: n.; *fōt*; foot: m.; *hand*; hand, f. While some exceptions occur, usually because of a conflict between grammatical and natural gender (e.g., Alfred writes in his translation of Boethius, while relating the story of Orpheus and Eurydice, *hē hæfde ān swiðe ǣnlic wif, sio wæs hāten Eurydice*; he had a wife without peer, who was called Eurydice, where the antecedent of the f. pron., *sio*, is the n. noun, *wif*.), in OE nouns, pronouns, and their modifiers or antecedents most frequently agree in number, gender, and, where applicable, case.

Occasionally, too, a subject and verb will not agree in number; look for collective nouns, or indefinite pronouns, to cause about the same difficulty as they do today. For example, Alfred, once again, in describing a curious custom which the voyager, Wulfstan, related to him, writes *and þonne rīdeð ǣlc hys weges mid ðǣm fēo, and hyt motan habban eall*; and then each rides his way towards the property, and (they) might have it all, where the singular forms *rīdeð ǣlc* do not appear to agree with the plural implication of *mōtan habban*. In these situations, obviously, Alfred was giving way to 'the feeling of the moment,' and the requirement for grammatical agreement was, happily, forgotten.

Articles

Since OE does not possess a distinctive, formal article, the demonstrative pronouns, *sē* and *þēs,* are used for 'the, that,' and 'this.' It should be observed, too, that OE will or will not display the demonstrative, so used, where, in MnE, we would not or would expect an article to occur. *Sē*, it should be recalled (examples occur in the texts given for these exercises), is also used as a relative pronoun.

Pronoun Reference

The third person pronoun frequently is used ambiguously; often it is difficult to determine to whom it refers. The well-known entry in *The Anglo-Saxon Chronicle* for the year 755 displays a bewildering array of loose third person pronoun references. We ourselves are sometimes guilty of similar lapses and should, therefore, impute this celebrated example of careless writing to its author, not to any flaw in the structure of OE.

Verbs

1. Since there is, with the single exception of *bēon*; be, no inflected form for the future tense in OE, the present tense forms are also used to signal the future; *ic ārīse and ic fare tō mīnum fæder and ic secge him*; I will arise and I will go to my father and I will say to him. *Ārīse, fare,* and *secge* are all 1 sg. pres. ind. forms, but the context in which they occur suggests future meaning. This situation, by the way, has not changed in MnE, which also has no formal future tense; the future is

formed by combining an auxilliary with an infinitive. We are able, too, to suggest future meaning by use of the simple present tense alone; 'I go to New York next week.' We permit 'I go today' and 'I go tomorrow,' but not '*I go yesterday.'

2. *Bēon* is conjugated in the present indicative as follows:

sg.	1	ic eom	I am	ic bēo	
	2	ðū eart	you are	ðū bist	
	3	hē is	he is	hē biþ	
pl.	1	wē sindon	we are	wē bēoþ	
	2	gē sindon	you are	gē bēoþ	
	3	hīe sindon	they are	gē bēoþ	

The *bēo* forms frequently are used for the future. The distinction between *ðū eart—ðū bist* and *gē sindon—gē bēoþ*, that is, the distinction between *ðū* and *gē*, has disappeared in MnE, where we make no formal distinction between second person singular and second person plural forms of the personal pronoun. We may translate the OE singular forms as 'thou art' and the plural forms as 'you are.'

3. The simple past tense (preterite) is used to signal a single action completed in the past or a continuing action in the past; *Sōþlīce þa þa menn slēpon, þa cōm his feonda sum*; Truly, when men slept (were sleeping), one of his enemies came.

4. Only one verb in OE, *hātan*, had an inflected passive voice form; *þæt wif hatte Wealhþēo*; the woman was called Wealhtheow. In all other instances, compound forms made by combining the past participle of the main verb with forms of *bēon, wesan,* or *weorþan* were used to construct the passive voice: with *bēon—bēon ðā oferhȳdegan ealle gescende*; may the proud be confounded; with *wesan—þæs gēares wǣrun ofslagen nigon eorlas*; nine earls were killed that year; with *weorþan —þæs gēares wurdon nigon folcgefeoht gefohton*; nine battles were fought that year.

A Few Constructions

The following constructions occur very frequently; their MnE equivalents, often governed by context, should be committed to memory.

æt niehstan, in the next place, thereupon
for hwon, why
for þǣm, for þām, therefore, because
for þǣm þe, for þām þe, because
for þan þe, therefore, because, for
for þon, forðon, therefore, because, for
for þon þe, for, because, therefore
for þȳ, for þȳ þe, therefore, because, for
mid þām þe, when, after, because
mid þȳ, mid þe, when, after, because
oððe . . . oððe, either . . . or
tō hwām, why
tō þæs þe, until
to þon þæt, in order that
þā . . . þā, when . . . then
þæs þe, since, afterwards, after, of which
þēah þe . . . þēah, although . . . nevertheless
þurh þæt þe, because

The grammatical information contained in the exercises on the selections from the earliest stage of our language, the Old English period (once again, from *ca.* 449, the traditional date for the advent of the Saxons in England to 1154, the date of the last entry in the Peterborough recension of *The Anglo-Saxon Chronicle*—although we represent it here as English of the year 1000), together with the grammatical hints given in various places in this section devoted to OE, is not, of course, all the information one needs to have to read Old English well. You might think of it as a slight, but firm, foundation. At some time in the future some of you will study Old English in greater depth, either with or without a teacher. If with a teacher, he will prescribe the text(s) to be used. For those who wish to carry out their own study many excellent texts are available. The short list here contains those texts which are both easily obtained and eminently helpful for the study of OE.

1. S. Moore and T. A. Knott. *The Elements of Old English.* 9th ed. Ann Arbor, Michigan: George Wahr, 1942.
2. J. R. Hulbert. *Bright's Anglo-Saxon Reader.* Latest ed. New York: Holt, 1947.
3. C. T. Onions. *Sweet's Anglo-Saxon Reader.* 14th ed. Oxford: The Clarendon Press, 1959.
4. A. J. Wyatt. *An Anglo-Saxon Reader.* Cambridge: Cambridge University Press, 1925.
5. R. C. Alston. *An Introduction to Old English.* Evanston, Ill.: Row, Peterson, 1962.
6. B. Mitchell. *A Guide to Old English.* Oxford: Basil Blackwell, 1965.
7. R. Quirk and C. L. Wrenn. *An Old English Grammar.* New York: Holt, Rinehart & Winston, 1957.
8. A. Campbell. *Old English Grammar.* Oxford: The Clarendon Press, 1959.

Number 1 is the easiest text to begin on; 2, 3, and 4 are anthologies, but 2 contains a useful 'Outline of Anglo-Saxon Grammar' and 'Sketch of Anglo-Saxon Literature'; 5 makes a good choice for a start because, in addition to the outline of grammar, it contains excellent exercises and a good description of syntax; 6 and 7 contain no reading selections but do contain admirable treatments of syntax—these two small books should be in the hands of all students of OE; 8, the most comprehensive grammar of OE, is the indispensible item on this list.

QUESTIONS

1. Without consulting the translation which follows these questions, translate the passage. Follow the same procedure established for the first two exercises.

2. Now study the translation which follows. You have two translations of this passage at hand; your own and the one which follows. Drawing on your own experience in writing translations, and making whatever use you can of the grammatical hints provided in these three exercises and in the glossaries, write a paper evaluating the Magoun-Walker translation. Your essay should take into consideration these points:

a. the purpose of translation

b. accurate reflection of the original text in balance with the style of the translation

c. conflicts caused, if any, by the translator having to choose (as King Alfred said about his own translations) between translating 'word by word' and translating 'sense to sense'

d. your opinion about the use of archaisms (attempt by translator to lend 'flavor of the past' to his work) in either structure or vocabulary in writing translations

e. the validity of 'supplying' what might appear to be missing in the original text

f. any other criteria you might add to help you to judge—to decide if a translation is good or bad

ÆLFRIC'S HOMILY ON THE ASSUMPTION
OF ST. JOHN THE EVANGELIST

Translated by F. P. Magoun, Jr., and J. A. Walker

John the Evangelist, favorite of Christ, was on this day (December 27th) through the visitation of God taken to the joy of the Kingdom of Heaven. He was the son of the sister of Christ's mother and the Latter loved him particularly (John 13: 23; 21: 7, 20), not so much because of the tie of kinship as for the purity of his perfect virginity. In (a state of) chastity he was chosen to God and to Eternity he remained in immaculate purity. One reads (lit. it is read) in authentic accounts that he was about to take a wife, and Christ was invited to his nuptials. Then it happened that at the nuptials (the) wine gave out. The Savior ordered the serving men to fill up six earthen-ware vessels with pure water and with His blessing He turned the water into very fine wine. This is the first miracle that He publicly performed during His Incarnation (John 2). Then John was so inspired by that miracle that then and there he left his bride in (a state of) virginity and ever after followed the Lord and was intensely loved by Him because he had snatched himself away from the lusts of the flesh. Indeed, to this beloved disciple the Savior entrusted His Mother when He redeemed mankind through the Crucifixion (lit. hanging on the Cross), so that the former's pure person might look after Mary the pure Virgin (cp. John 19: 27). And she then remained in the household of her sister's son.

In turn in time, after Christ's Ascension into Heaven, there ruled in the Roman Empire after Nero a certain blood-thirsty emperor. He was called Domitian (regn. 81–96 A.D.), a persecutor of all Christian persons; he ordered a tub to be filled with boiling oil and the illustrious evangelist to be thrust into it. However, through the protection of God he came out of that hot bath unharmed. Again, when that blood-thirsty man was unable to suppress the Blessed Apostle's preaching, then he sent him into exile to an island that is called Patmos, so that there he might die through the pangs (lit. sharpness) of hunger. But the Almighty Savior did not in too neglectful fashion abandon His beloved Apostle but revealed to him in that exile the revelation of the future, according to which he wrote that book which is called Apocalypse (cp. Rev. 1: 9). And the blood-thirsty Domitian in that same year (A.D. 96) was slain at the hands of his senators (historically by a freedman Stephanus), and they all unanimously advised that all the latter's decrees be invalidated. Then Nerva (regn. 96–98 A.D.), a most virtuous man, was chosen emperor. By his permission the Apostle returned again (to Rome) with great honor, he who had in insulting fashion been sent into exile. Men and women ran to meet him, rejoicing and saying, "Blessed is he who has come in the name of the Lord."

As the Apostle John was entering the city of Ephesus (mod. Ayasuluk), then people were carrying in his direction the body of a widow to be buried; her name was Drusiana. She was a staunch believer and charitable, and the needy whom she with generous spirit had entirely supported, sad followed the corpse weeping (lit. with weeping). Then the Apostle ordered the beir to be set down and said, "May My Lord Savior raise you up, Drusiana; arise and go home and prepare a meal for us in your house." Then Drusiana arose as if awakened from sleep and, mindful of the Apostle's command, went home.

✠ ✠ ✠

TRANSITION

One passage has been selected to illustrate the quality of prose produced at about the year 1200, midway between the best of Old English prose and the mature compositions of the Middle English period. This is the text:

4. *Ancrene Wisse.* Written probably in the last quarter of the twelfth century, this "Rule for Anchoresses" clearly shows that its author possessed an extremely sensitive insight and depth of human sympathy, and, what is more, that he was master of an elegant, forceful prose style. The entire work was first published by James Morton (*The Ancren Riwle,* Camden Society No. LVII, London, 1853).

THE LOVE OF CHRIST

Ancrene Wisse, ca. 1170–1200

lines 1–68

3. THE LOVE OF CHRIST

A leafdi wes mid hire fan biset al abuten, hire lond al
destruet ant heo al povre, inwið an eorðene castel, A mihti
kinges luve wes þah biturnd upon hire, swa unimete swiðe
þet he for wohlech sende hire his sonden, an efter oðer, ofte
somet monie, sende hire beawbelex baðe feole and feire,   5
sucurs of liveneð, help of his hehe hird to halden hire castel.
Heo underfeng al as on unrecheles ant swa wes heard
i-heortet þet hire luve ne mahte he neaver beo þe neorre.
Hwet wult tu mare? He com himseolf on ende, schawde
hire his feire neb, as þe þe wes of alle men fehrest to bihal-   10
den, spec se swiðe swoteliche ant wordes se murie þet ha
mahten deade arearen to live, wrahte feole wundres ant dude
muchele meistrics bivoren hire ehsihðe, schawde hire his
mihte, talde hire of his kinedom, bead to makien hire cwen
ot al þet he ahte. Al þis ne heold nawt. Nes þis hoker   15
wunder? For heo nes neaver wurðe for to beon his þuften.
Ah swa, þurh his deboneirte, luve hefde overcumen him þet
he seide on ende· 'Dame, þu art i-weorret, ant þine van
beoð se stronge þet tu ne maht nanes-weis, wiðute mi sucurs
edfleon hare honden, þet ha ne don þe to scheome deað efter   20
al þi weane. Ich chulle, for þc luve of þe, neome þet feht upo
me, ant arudde þe of ham þe þi deað sechcð. Ich wat þah
to soðe þet ich schal bituhen ham neomen deaðes wunde:
ant ich hit wulle heorteliche for te ofgan þin heorte. Nu
þenne, biseche ich þe, for þe luve þet ich cuðe þe, þet tu   25
luvie me lanhure efter þe ilke deað, hwen þu naldest lives!'
Þes king dude al þus, arudde hire of alle hire van, ant wes
himseolf to wundre i-tuket, ant i-slein on ende. Þurh miracle
aras þah from deaðe to live. Nere þeos ilke leafdi of uveles
cunnes cunde, ȝef ha over alle þing ne luvede him herefter?   30
    Þes king is Jesu, Godes sune, þet al o þisse wise wohede
ure sawle þe deoflen hefden bihest. Ant he, as noble wohere
efter monie messagers ant feole god deden, com to pruvien

Reprinted from F. Mossé, *A Handbook of Middle English*, J. A. Walker (tr.) (Baltimore: The
Johns Hopkins Press, 1952), pp. 142–147, by permission of the publisher. The translation to
Modern English which follows is Alan M. Markman's.

his luve, and schawde þurh cnihtschipe þet he was luve-
wurðe, as weren sumhwile cnihtes i-wunet to donne, dude   *35*
him i turneiment ant hefde for his leoves luve his scheld i
feht, as kene cniht, on euche half i-þurlet. His scheld þe
wreah his Goddhead wes his leove licome þet wes i-spread o
rode, brad as scheld buven in his i-strahte earmes, nearow
bineoðen, as þe an fot, efter monies wene, set upo þe oðer.   *40*
Þet þis scheld naveð siden is for bitacnunge þet his deciples,
þe schulden stonden bu him ant habben i-beon his siden,
fluhen alle from him ant leafden him as fremede as þe
godspel seið: *Relicto eo, omnes fugerunt.* Þis scheld is
i-ȝeven us aȝein alle temptatiuns, as Jeremie witneð: *Dabis*   *45*
scutum cordis laborem tuum. Nawt ane þis scheld ne schilt
us from alle uveles ah deð ȝet mare, cruneð us in heovene:
Scuto bonae voluntatis. 'Laverd,' he seið, Davið, 'wið þe
scheld of þi gode wil þu havest us i-crunet.' Scheld, he seið,
of god wil; for willes he þolede al þet he þolede. Ysaias: *50*
Oblatus est quia voluit. 'Me, Laverd,' þu seist, 'hwerto? Ne
mahte he wið leasse gref habben arud us?' ȝeoi, i-wis, ful
lihtlice; ah he nalde. For-hwi? For to bineomen us euch
bitellunge aȝein him of ure luve, þet he se deore bohte. Me
buð lihtliche þing þet me luveð lutel. He bohte us wið his   *55*
heorte blod, deorre pris nes neaver, for te ofdrahen of us ure
luve toward him þet costnede him se sare. I scheld beoð
þreo þinges, þe treo ant te leðer ant te litunge. Alswa wes i
þis scheld þe treo of þe rode, þet leðer of Godes licome, þe
litunge of þe reade blod þet heowede hire se feire. Eft, þe   *60*
þridde reisun: Efter kene cnihtes deað, me hongeð hehe i
chirche his scheld on his mungunge. Alswa is þis scheld, þet
is þe crucifix, i chirche i-set i swuch stude þer me hit sonest
seo, for te þenchen þerbi o Jesu Cristes cnihtschipe þet he
dude o rode. His leofmon bihalde þron hu he bohte hire   *65*
luve, lette þurlin his scheld, openin his side, to schawin hire
his heorte, to schawin hire openliche hu inwardliche he
luvede hire ant to ofdrahen hire heorte.

This text is translated, quite literally, word for word in this way:

A lady was with her enemies beset all about, her land all
destroyed and she all poor, within an earthen castle. A mighty
king's love was however turned towards her, so immeasurably very
that he for courting sent her his messengers, one after other, often
together many, sent her baubles both many and fair,   *5*
help of living, help of his high court to hold her castle.
She received all as one careless and so was hard
hearted that her love not might he never be the nearer.
What wilt thou more? He came himself on end, showed
her his fair face, as he who was of all men fairest to behold,   *10*
spoke so exceedingly sweetly and words so merry that they

might the dead raise to life, wrought many wonders and did
great marvels before her eyesight, showed her his
might, told her of his kingdom, bade to make her queen
of all that he owned. All this not held naught. Not was this scorn   15
marvelous? For she not was never worthy for to be his slave.
But so, through his debonairness, love had overcome him that
he said on end: "Madam, you are attacked, and thy foes
be so strong that you not might not at all, without my help
escape their hands, that they not do thee to ashamed death after   20
all thy misery. I shall, for the love of thee, take that fight upon
me, and save thee from them who thy death seek. I know though
in truth that I shall between them take death's wound:
and I it wish heartily for to obtain thine heart. Now
then, beseech I thee, for the love that I made known to thee, that you   25
love me at least after the same death when you would not while alive!"
This king did all thus, saved her from all her enemies, and was
himself terribly mistreated, and slain at the end. Through a miracle
arose though from death to life. Not were this same lady of evils
kinds nature, if she over all matters not loved him hereafter?   30
This king is Jesus, God's son, who completely in this manner courted
our souls which devils had besieged. And he, as a great wooer
after many messengers and many good deeds, came to prove
his love, and showed through knightship that he was worthy of love
as were sometime knights accustomed to do, did   35
him in tournament and had for his beloved's love his shield in
a combat, as a bold knight, on each side pierced. His shield which
covered his Godhead was his dear body that was stretched out on
the cross, broad as a shield above in his stretched out arms, narrow
below, as the one foot, for the hopes of many, was placed over the other.   40
That this shield not has sides is for betokening that his disciples,
who should stand by him and have been his sides,
fled all from him and left him as foreign as the
gospel says: *Relicto eo, omnes fugerunt.* This shield is
given us against all temptations, as Jeremiah witnesses: *Dabis*   45
scutum cordis laborem tuum. Not only this shield not shields
us from all evils but does yet more, crowns us in heaven:
scuto bonæ voluntatis. "Lord," he says, David, "with the
shield of thy goodness will you have us crowned." Shield, he says,
of good will; for of will he suffered all that he suffered. Isaiah: 50
Oblatus est quia voluit. 'Me,' Lord, you say, 'why?' Not
might he with less grief have saved us? Yes, certainly, for sure, very
easily, but he not would. Why? For to deprive us each
excuse against him of our love, that he so dearly purchased. It
purchases to me lightly thing that to me loves little. He bought us with his   55
heart's blood, dearer prize not was never, for to draw from us our
love toward him that cost him so sorely. In the shield are
three things, the tree and the leather and the color. At the same time was in
this shield the tree of the cross, the leather of God's body, the
color of the red blood that colored her so fairly. Finally, the   60

third reason: After bold knight's death, men hang high in
church his shield in his memory. At the same time is this shield, that
is the crucifix, in church placed in such place there where men it soonest
see, for to think thereby on Jesus Christ's knightship that he
did on cross. Let his dearly beloved behold thereon how he bought her   65
love, permitted to pierce his shield, open his side, to show her
his heart, to show her openly how inwardly he
loved her and to draw off her heart.

QUESTIONS

Roughly two centuries separate this text from the OE texts you have read. To
perceive the nature of the changes in the language during that time, you might well
begin by considering the phenomenon of *levelling*. When the full inflectional system
of OE started to give way to the system of grammatical signals employed in MnE,
certain inflectional endings weakened, eventually to be replaced by word order
signals or function words. One development to be observed is the loss of final *-n*.
In OE the infinitive of the verb ended in *-an* or *-ian*. In this passage, however, the
usual infinitive ending is *-en*, and for weak verbs *-in* (*openin*, l. 66, *þurlin*, l. 66,
schawin, l. 67) or *-ien* (*makien*, l. 14). In OE the vowel of the infinitive ending had
the sound of the vowel in MnE 'hot' or 'box' and was stressed. What probably
occurred is that as stress weakened on the vowel of the infinitive ending it came to be
sounded as the first vowel in MnE 'about' is sounded, and as stress weakened further
the vowel, in its written representation, came to be spelled as it is in this text with *e*,
and the final *-n* was also subjected to weakened stress. Eventually the final *-n*
disappeared (as even earlier final *-m* changed to *-n*) and the final *-e* thus left also, in
time, disappeared. In this text, however, only the first step can be observed; the
change of the vowel of the inflectional ending has occurred, but the final *-n* is still
retained. But we can project this process:

900	1200	MnE
behealdan	bihalden	behold

Something of this identical feature can be observed in prepositions in this text,
where, with weakened or no stress, *in* and *on* are printed as *i* and *o*. MnE, of course,
has retained 'in' and 'on.' There also are numerous noun plurals in this text which
end in *-en*, all of which will, in the next few centuries, lose that inflection and adopt
the final *-s* as the signal of the plural. (A few exceptions to that general development
remain in MnE; 'ox' and 'child,' for example.) Your later texts, from the late ME
and the EMnE periods will show further stages of levelling. While examining this
passage it will prove helpful, as you consider in what ways the English of 1200
differs from the English of 1000, to look for evidence of early levelling and the con-
sequent appearance of other grammatical signals replacing the inflectional functions.

1. Rewrite the passage in your own compositional style.

2. Here is a series of questions designed to illustrate some of the distinctive
features of this text.

a. *deade*, l. 12, is a pl. adj.; how is it used here?

b. *leoves,* 1. 36, is an adj. in the gen. case; how is it used here?

c. what is the number of *þing* in 1. 30?

d. what is the construction of *deaðes* in 1. 23?

e. what is the construction and function of *hire* in 1. 60?

f. *me,* in 1. 54 and 55, is dat.; what is its function?

g. *fremede,* 1. 43, is an adj.; what is its function?

h. forms of *do* occur in 1. 12, 20, 27, 35, and 65; what are their functions?

i. does *to* ever occur (in front of the verb) as the signal of the infinitive? If so, what does that suggest?

j. are there any superfluous negative particles in the text?

k. *þe* can mean 'the' or 'thee'; how are its meanings distinguished?

3. Summarize your findings regarding the changes which took place in the English language between 900 and 1200.

✠ ✠ ✠

MIDDLE ENGLISH
1150–1471

Here too it is not possible to assign exact dates for the beginning and end of this stage in the development of our language. Indeed, as it will become obvious once all the texts have been examined, clearly defined limits, or boundaries, marking off one level of the development of language from another do not exist. Changes in language occur slowly, over the spread of generations, as a result of various pressures and forces exerted upon the speakers. A vast, complex matrix of political, economic, and social mobilities erodes, most often as scarcely noticeable sorties, sometimes as radical upheavals, those conservative popular barriers which resist change. In this period, of course, the victory which William the Conqueror long ago gained over Harold Godwinson at the Battle of Hastings in 1066 was the most significant cause for change, because, as a result, in the generations that followed, thousands upon thousands of speakers of Anglo-Norman French spread over the lands of Britain, eventually to mingle with the Saxons and to produce, in time, speakers of a new, more resourceful English. In the fourteenth century—the height of the period— English writers produced a world famous literature, still widely read, its authors, some anonymous, some known to us, still admired. Again, for the sake of convenience, we choose the middle of the twelfth century to mark the start of the Middle English period and the death of Malory, 1471 (roughly equivalent, too, with Caxton and the introduction of printing into Britain), to signal its close.

To represent Middle English we have selected three texts which illustrate English of the year 1400, the year in which Chaucer died. Two of the selections are the work of Chaucer; the third, while not clearly established as his, might be from his hand. These are the texts:

5. *The Canterbury Tales*. Geoffrey Chaucer, 1385. From the *General Prologue*, the 'portrait' of the Prioress constitutes a sample of superior composition, in verse, in Middle English.

6. *The Romaunt of the Rose*. Chaucer (?), 1370. This passage, in verse, is a translation into Middle English of a great twelfth century Old French poem.

7. *A Treatise on the Astrolabe*. Geoffrey Chaucer, 1385. The opening paragraphs of this work (as arranged by modern editors) illustrate the achievement of Middle English prose.

EXERCISE 5
THE CANTERBURY TALES
Chaucer, ca. 1385
A, 118–162

GENERAL PROLOGUE, PORTRAIT OF THE PRIORESS

Ther was also a Nonne, a Prioresse,
That of hir smyling was ful simple and coy;
Hir gretteste ooth was but by seynte Loy;   *120*
And she was cleped madame Eglentyne.
Ful wel she song the service divyne,
Entuned in hir nose ful semely;
And Frensh she spak ful faire and fetisly,
After the scole of Stratford atte Bowe,   *125*
For Frensh of Paris was to hir unknowe.
At mete wel y-taught was she with-alle;
She leet no morsel from hir lippes falle,
Ne wette hir fingres in hir sauce depe.
Wel coude she carie a morsel, and wel kepe,   *130*
That no drope ne fille up-on hir brest.
In curteisye was set ful muche hir lest.
Hir over lippe wyped she so clene,
That in hir coppe was no ferthing sene
Of grece, whan she dronken hadde hir draughte.   *135*
Ful semely after hir mete she raughte,
And sikerly she was of greet disport,
And ful plesaunt, and amiable of port,
And peyned hir to countrefete chere
Of court, and been estatlich of manere,   *140*
And to ben holden digne of reverence.
But, for to speken of hir conscience,
She was so charitable and so pitous,
She wolde wepe, if that she sawe a mous
Caught in a trappe, if it were deed or bledde.   *145*
Of smale houndes had she, that she fedde
With rosted flesh, or milk and wastel-breed.
But sore weep she if oon of hem were deed,
Or if men smoot it with a yerde smerte:
And al was conscience and tendre herte.   *150*
Ful semely hir wimpel pinched was;
Hir nose tretys; hir eyen greye as glas;

Hir mouth ful smal, and ther-to softe and reed;
But sikerly she hadde a fair forheed;
It was almost a spanne brood, I trowe; *155*
For, hardily, she was nat undergrowe.
Ful fetis was hir cloke, as I was war.
Of smal coral aboute hir arm she bar
A peire of bedes, gauded al with grene;
And ther-on heng a broche of gold ful shene, *160*
On which ther was first write a crowned A,
And after, *Amor vincit omnia.*

GLOSSARY

In this listing will be found only words which are unfamiliar in contemporary English; they are cited in alphabetical order with the line number from this text.

cleped, called: 121.
countrefete, imitate: 139.
digne, worthy: 141.
estatlich, stately, royal: 140.
ferthing, bit, small piece: 134.
fetis, skilfull: 157.
fetisly, skilfully: 124.
flesh, meat. 147.
gauded, dyed, enameled: 159.
lest, desire, wish: 132.
mete, meat, the dining table: 127.

peyned, took pains: 139.
pinched, pleated: 151.
raughte, reached: 136.
scole, school: 125.
semely, fashionably: 123, 151.
shene, beautiful, glittering: 160.
sikerly, truly, indeed: 137, 154.
smerte, smartly: 149.
tretys, straight, well made: 152.
yerde, stick: 149.

QUESTIONS

1. Translate the passage. The glossary provides meanings for all words which have not retained their same meaning in MnE or which, in their ME spelling, look in some way odd to us. Make a comparison of Chaucer's syntax with MnE practise, allowing, of course, for the fact that this is a passage of poetry. In your remarks include a statement about the use of adjectives, i.e., the position of the adj. (in ll. 121, 129, 146, 147, 152, 154) with regard to the noun it modifies. Is the use of *tretys,* l. 152, of the same order as the others?

2. In the language of 1400 we should expect a certain number of French loan words to occur. A *loan word* is one appearing in one language, which is not a native word but which has been borrowed from another language. English has been a good borrower. Make a chart on the model shown below in which you place each word (in its MnE form) from the text (only of the classes indicated, the four principal parts of speech). Consult the *OED,* or an unabridged dictionary, to determine which are French loan words.

	Noun	Verb	Adj.	Adv.
118	nun	was		also
	prioress			
119	smiling	was	simple	full
			coy	
120	oath	was	greatest	
	saint			

Complete your chart. What is the percentage of French loan words in the text? In what part of speech was borrowing heaviest? How can you determine if a word had been borrowed by French from Latin and then from French by English? Would you call such an example an English borrowing from French?

3. Inflectional levelling has proceeded further than it had by the year 1200. Make a list of all plural nouns which occur in the text. What is the normal inflection? How do you account for the form of the plural noun in 1. 152? What is the MnE form for each of these words? Can you explain how the MnE form developed?

4. You will have observed that a good many of the words in this text end in a final -e. The final -e in the English of 1400 has in the past been the subject of much inquiry and concern. Was it pronounced? If it was not pronounced we can state that it had no significance, i.e., if in normal conversation it was not heard, then no signal was uttered. If pronounced, was it a grammatical signal? We can determine if the final -e in this text is to be pronounced by scanning the lines of verse. We assume that Chaucer's metrical skill is superior and that, intending to write iambic pentameter in this passage, he was not likely to make errors. Confine the inquiry now to singular nouns ending in final -e. There are two in the first line. The line may be scanned in this way:

thĕr wás ăl só ă Nónne ă Prí ŏr ésse

Since no marker appears over the final -e's, it is evident that neither was pronounced. Make a similar test for each singular noun in the text and place all the nouns which show a pronounced final -e in a list. (Mete, 1. 127, for example, has a pronounced final -e: ăt mé tĕ wél y̆ taúght . . .) Consult the OED for the origin of each word on your list. If you find a loan word, how would you regard the pronounced final -e? If a native English word, how would you regard it? What has happened in MnE to each of these words? (Try to establish a distinction between a derivational, or etymological, ending and an inflectional ending.) Can you, finally, make a general statement, using just this text as evidence, about the final -e in Chaucer's poetry: when is it pronounced and when is it not? (When pronounced, it has the sound of the first vowel in MnE 'about.')

THE ROMAUNT OF THE ROSE

Chaucer, lines 1–40, ca. 1370

Many men sayn that in sweveninges
Ther nys but fables and lesynges;
But men may some swevenes sene
Whiche hardely that false ne bene,
But afterwarde ben apparaunt.   *5*
This maye I drawe to warraunt
An authour that hight Macrobes,
That halte nat dremes false ne lees,
But undothe us the avysioun
That whilom mette kyng Ciploun.   *10*
And who-so saith, or weneth it be
A jape, or elles nycete,
To wene that dremes after falle,
Lette who so lyste a fole me calle.
For this trowe I, and say for me,   *15*
That dremes signifiaunce be
Of good and harme to many wightes,
That dremen in her slepe a nyghtes
Ful many thynges covertly,
That fallen after al openly.   *20*
Within my twenty yere of age,
Whan that Love taketh his cariage
Of yonge folke, I wente soone
To bedde, as I was wont to done,
And faste I slepte; and in slepyng   *25*
Me mette suche a swevenyng
That lyked me wonder wele.
But in that sweven is never a dele
That it nys afterwarde befalle,
Ryght as this dreme wol tel us alle.   *30*
Nowe this dreme wol I ryme a-right,
To make your hertes gaye and lyght,
For Love it prayeth and also
Commaundeth me that it be so.
And if there any aske me,   *35*
Whether that it be he or she,
Howe this booke whiche is here
Shal hatte, that I rede you here;
It is the Romance of the Rose,
In whiche al the Arte of Love I close.   *40*

GLOSSARY

Here is a list of all words which might prove troublesome.

close, disclose: 40.
dele, part, bit: 28.
hatte, be called: 38.
hight, is called: 7.
jape, joke: 12.
lesynges, lies: 2.
lyste, please, like: 14.

mette, dreamed: 26.
nycete, a foolishness: 12.
rede, advise: 38.
sweveninges, dreams: 1.
trowe, believe: 15.
undothe, discloses: 9.
wightes, persons: 17.

QUESTIONS

1. Translate this passage.

2. From this text and the text for Exercise 5 make a list of all the personal pronouns which occur. What is the form of the 3d sg. fem. gen.? Its MnE equivalent is 'her.' The corresponding form in OE was *hire*; can you account for the evolution of 'her'? In 1. 148, Exercise 5, *hem* occurs and in this text, 1. 18, *her* occurs; what is the construction of each? Consult the *OED* to determine the source of the MnE equivalents. What does this suggest about English lexical borrowing habits?

3. From this text and the text for Exercise 5 make a list of all verbal constructions. Place your examples into a paradigmatic format. Compare each inflectional form with its OE and MnE counterparts. What has been the development of these forms since the end of the OE period? In Exercise 5, 1. 127, the form *y-taught* occurs. Consult the *OED* for the orgin of the prefix *y-*. What was the normal signal for the past participle in OE? in these ME texts?

EXERCISE 7
A TREATISE ON THE ASTROLABE
Chaucer, ca. 1385, lines 1–39

Lyte Lowys my sone, I aperceyve wel by certeyne evydences thyn abilite to lerne
sciences touching nombres and proporciouns; and as wel considre I thy bisy
praier in special to lerne the Tretys of the Astrelabie. Than for as mochel as a
philosofre saith, 'he wrappith him in his frende, that condescendith to the
rightful praiers of his frende,' therefore have I yeven the a suffisant Astrolabie   5
as for oure orizonte compowned after the latitude of Oxenford; upon which, by
mediacioun of this litel tretys, I propose to teche the a certein nombre of
conclusions perteynyng to the same instrument. I seie a certein of conclusions
for thre causes. The first cause is this: truste wel that alle the conclusions that
han be founde, or ellys possibly might be founde in so noble an instrument as   10
is an Astrelabie ben unknowe parfitly to eny mortal man in this regioun, as I
suppose. Another cause is this, that sothly in any tretis of the Astrelabie that I
have sene there be somme conclusions that wol not in alle thinges parformen
her bihestes; and somme of hem ben to harde to thy tendir age of x yere to
conceyve.   15
   This tretis, divided in 5 parties, wol I shewe the under full light reules and
naked wordes in Englisshe, for Latyn canst thou yit but small, my litel sone.
But natheles suffise to the these trewe conclusions in Englisshe as wel as
sufficith to these noble clerkes Grekes these same conclusions in Greke; and to
Arabiens in Arabike, and to Iewes in Ebrewe, and to the Latyn folk in Latyn;   20
whiche Latyn folke had hem first oute of othere dyverse langages, and writen
hem in her owne tunge, that is to seyn in Latyn. And God woot that in alle these
langages and in many moo han these conclusions ben suffisantly lerned and
taught, and yit by diveres reules; right as diverse pathes leden diverse folke the
right way to Rome. Now wol I preie mekely every discret persone that redith or   25
herith this litel tretys to have my rude endityng for excused, and my superfluite
of wordes, for two causes. The first cause is for that curiouse endityng and harde
sentence is ful hevy at onys for such a childe to lerne. And the secunde cause is
this, that sothly me semith better to writen unto a childe twyes a gode sentence,
than he forgete it onys.   30
   And Lowys, yf so be that I shewe the in my light Englisshe as trewe conclusions touching this mater, and not oonly as trewe but as many and as subtile
conclusiouns, as ben shewid in Latyn in eny commune tretys of the Astrelabie,
konne me the more thanke. And preie God save the King, that is lorde of this
langage, and alle that him feithe berith and obeieth, everiche in his degre, the   35
more and the lasse. But considre wel that I ne usurpe not to have founden this
werke of my labour or of myn engyn. I nam but a lewde compilator of the
labour of olde astrologiens, and have it translatid in myn Englisshe oonly for
thy doctrine. And with this swerde shal I sleen envie.

GLOSSARY

endityng, writing: 27.
engyn, ingenuity: 37.
founden, invented: 36.
sentence, meaning: 28 (in 29 read MnE 'sentence').

QUESTIONS

1. Translate the passage.

2. Employing all the techniques encountered so far in previous exercises, write a paper comparing Chaucer's prose with Aelfric's.

3. Read further in an edition of Chaucer's complete works from "The Parson's Tale" and "The Tale of Melibeus" for a larger sampling of Chaucer's prose. In what respect might you say that Chaucer is or is not a more "modern" writer than Aelfric?

✠ ✠ ✠

TRANSITION

One passage has been selected to illustrate the quality of prose produced midway between the end of the thirteenth century and the close of the fifteenth. Caxton's modernization of Trevisa's translation of *Polychronicon Ranulphi Higden,* which he printed in 1482, serves this purpose and one other too: it provides, as well, a contemporary observation on the English language. But it must be remembered, Higden died in 1364, and John of Trevisa's translation was finished in 1387. Therefore, while the style of this text is Caxton's, and the language in which it is written is the English of 1482, the content reflects the condition of English in 1387, in the period, that is, of Chaucer's mature expression. This is the text:

8. *Polychronicon.* Caxton, 1482. Fifty lines and a partial glossary are provided.

MODERNIZATION AND PRINTING OF JOHN
OF TREVISA'S TRANSLATION OF HIGDEN'S
POLYCHRONICON
William Caxton, lines 1–49, 1482

As it is knowen how many maner peple ben in this Ilond ther ben also many
langages and tonges. Netheles walshmen and scottes that ben not medled with
other nacions kepe neygh yet theyr first langage and speche/ But yet tho scottes
that were sometyme confederate and dwellyd with pyctes drawe somwhat after
theyr speche/ But the Flemynges that dwelle in the westside of wales have lefte   5
her straunge speche & speken lyke to saxons/ also englysshmen though they had
fro the begynnyng thre maner speches Southern northern and myddel speche in
the middel of the londe as they come of thre maner of people of Germania.
Netheles by commyxtion and medlyng with danes and afterward with normans
In many thynges the countreye langage is appayred/ffor somme use straunge   10
wlaffyng/chyteryng harryng garryng and grisbytyng/ this appayryng of the
langage cometh of two thynges/One is by cause that children that gon to scole
lerne to speke first englysshe/& than ben compellid to constrewe her lessons in
Frenssh and that have ben used syn the normans come in to Englond/Also
gentilmens childeren ben lerned and taught from theyr yongthe to speke   15
frenssh.

And uplondish men will counterfete and likene hem self to gentilmen and arn
besy to speke frensshe for to be more sette by. Wherfor it is sayd by a comyn
proverbe Jack wold be a gentilman if he coude speke frensshe. This manner
was moche used to fore the grete deth. But syth it is somdele chaunged For sir   20
Johan cornuayl a mayster of gramer chaunged the techyng in gramer scole and
construction of Frenssh in to englysshe. and other Schoolmaysters use the same
way now in the yere of oure lord/M.iij/C.lx.v. the /IX yere of kyng Rychard the
secund and leve all frenssh in scoles and use al construction in englisshe. wherein
they have avantage one way. that is that they lerne the sonner theyr gramer And   25
in another disavauntage/For nowe they lerne no ffrenssh ne can none/whiche is
hurte for them that shal passe the see/And also gentilmen have moche lefte to
teche theyr children to speke frenssh Hit semeth a grete wonder that Englyssmen
have so grete dyversyte in theyr owne langage in sowne and in spekyng of it/
whiche is all in one ylond. And the langage of Normandye is comen oute of   30
another lond/and hath one manner soune among al men that speketh it in
englond For a man of Kente Southern/ western and northern men speken
Frensshe al lyke in sowne & speche. But they can not speke theyr englyssh so
Netheles ther is as many dyverse manere of Frensshe in the Royamme of
Fraunce as is dyverse englysshe in the Royamme of Engelond Also of the   35

Reprinted from F. Mossé, *A Handbook of Middle English*, J. A. Walker (tr.) (Baltimore: The
Johns Hopkins Press, 1952), pp. 286–289, by permission of the publisher.

forsayd tong whiche is departed in thre is grete wonder/For men of the este
with the men of the west acorde better in sownyng of theyr speche than men of
the north with men of the south/

Therfor it is that men of mercij that ben of myddel englond as it were
partyners with the endes understande better the side langages northern &   *40*
sothern than northern & southern understande eyther other. Alle the langages
of the northumbres & specially at york is so sharp slytyng frotyng and unshape
that we sothern men may unneth understande that langage I suppose the cause
be that they be nygh to the alyens that speke straungely. And also by cause that
the kynges of englond abyde and dwelle more in the south countreye than in   *45*
the north countrey.

The cause why they abyde more in the south countrey than in the north
countrey. is by cause that ther is better corne londe more peple moo noble
cytees. & moo prouffytable havenes in the south contrey than in the north.

GLOSSARY

alyens, aliens: 44.
appayred, deteriorated: 10.
appayryng, deterioration: 11.
can, know: 26: are able: 33.
chyteryng, chattering: 11.
corne, wheat, grain: 48.
frotyng, grinding: 42.
garryng, grating: 11.

grete deth, the mid-fourteenth-century plague: 20.
grisbytyng, grinding the teeth: 11.
harryng, snarling: 11.
havenes, harbors: 49.
mercij, Mercia: 39.
slytyng, piercing: 42.
unneth, not easily: 43.
wlaffyng, stammering: 11.

QUESTIONS

This passage was written at a time roughly half way between the productions of
Chaucer and those of Shakespeare. The fifteenth century frequently has been called
'the century of transition.' We should expect the English of 1482 to display some
traces of its ME heritage and, at the same time, to show some resemblance to what,
yet, lies ahead.

1. List all the verb, noun, and pronoun constructions. Has levelling proceeded
further than it had at 1400? What percentage (roughly) of final -*n* forms occur?

2. What is the form of the future tense here?

3. The *virgule* (a short oblique stroke, /, which we today sometimes use between
two words to suggest that either interpretation may be used, as in 'and/or') was,
on occasion, used by early printers to mark the end of word groups. What is its
relationship to modern punctuation marks? Does it suggest anything about pronunciation or pauses?

4. If you were to prepare a modernized edition of this passage, what changes
would you make?

5. Do you regard this passage in any way to be an advance over Chaucer's
prose?

✠ ✠ ✠

EARLY MODERN ENGLISH

1500–1700

By the beginning of the sixteenth century, owing to the increased production of books made possible by the activities of the printers and their presses, and to a marked rise in volume of written communication in general, it is evident that a new stage in the development of English had been reached. While the English language of 1500 does not yet look, in its written form, like ours, nor in its oral production could it yet have sounded like ours, it is clear, nevertheless, that English was embarking upon a new series of changes, which, over the course of two centuries, were destined to leave an indelible trace upon it. It is in this period, of course, that two of the greatest poets England has produced, Shakespeare and Milton, lived and wrote their works. It was a period of great bustle, intense social activity, and a general expansion of man's inquiry and action everywhere. And the English language, borrowing here, adapting there, became a flexible medium of expression, sufficiently versatile to sustain all the needs of communication which attended the largest burst of human energy the world had up to that time witnessed. While the limits are, once again, hard to fix, we are safe enough in choosing 1500 as the start and 1700, the year of the death of Dryden, a writer whose works display most of the features of Modern English, as the close of the most vigorous period in the history of our language.

We have selected three passages from Shakespeare, two in verse and one (partially) in prose, to represent the Early Modern English period. These are the texts:

9. *As You Like It*. This passage is reproduced as it was printed in the 1623 Folio Edition.

10. *Romeo and Juliet*. The printing of the 1623 Folio Edition is used.

11. *Hamlet*. This text is taken from a modern edition.

EXERCISE 9
AS YOU LIKE IT
I. iii. 43–111, Shakespeare, 1623 Folio

DUK. Mistris, dispatch you with your fastest haste,
    And get you from our Court.
ROS. Me Vncle?
DUK. You Cosen,
    Within these ten daies if that thou beest found   *45*
    So neere our publike Court as twentie miles,
    Thou diest for it.
ROS. I doe beseech your Grace
    Let me the knowledge of my fault beare with me:
    If with my selfe I hold intelligence,   *50*
    Or haue acquaintance with mine owne desires,
    If that I doe not dreame, or be not franticke,
    (As I doe trust I am not) then deere Vncle,
    Neuer so much as in a thought vnborne,
    Did I offend your highnesse.   *55*
DUK. Thus doe all Traitors,
    If their purgation did consist in words,
    They are as innocent as grace itselfe;
    Let it suffice thee that I trust thee not.
ROS. Yet your mistrust cannot make me a Traitor;   *60*
    Tell me whereon the likelihoods depends?
DUK. Thou art thy Fathers daughter, there's enough.
ROS. So was I when your highness took his Dukedom,
    So was I when your highness banisht him;
    Treason is not inherited my Lord,   *65*
    Or if we did deriue it from our friends,
    What's that to me, my Father was no Traitor,
    Then good my Leige, mistake me not so much,
    To thinke my pouertie is treacherous.
CEL. Deere Soueraigne heare me speake.   *70*
DUK. I Celia, we staid her for your sake,
    Else had she with her Father rang'd along.
CEL. I did not then entreat to haue her stay,
    It was your pleasure, and your owne remorse,
    I was too yong that time to value her,   *75*
    But now I know her: if she be a Traitor,
    Why so am I: we still haue slept together
    Rose at an instant, learn'd, plaid, eate together,

Reprinted from Albert H. Marckwardt, *Introduction to the English Language* (New York: Oxford University Press, 1942), by permission of the publisher.

And wheresoere we went, like *Iunos* Swans,
Still we went coupled and inseperable.   *80*
DUK. She is too subtile for thee, and her smoothness;
Her verie silence, and (h)er patience,
Speake to the people, and they pittie her:
Thou art a foole, she robs thee of thy name,
And thou wilt show more bright, & seem more vertuous
When she is gone: then open not thy lips   *85*
Firme, and irreuocable is my doombe,
Which I haue past vpon her, she is banish'd.
CEL. Pronounce that sentence then on me my Leige,
I cannot liue out of her companie.
DUK. You are a foole: you Neice prouide your selfe,   *90*
If you out-stay the time, vpon mine honor,
And in the greatnesse of my word you die.

                                                      Exit Duke, etc.

CEL. O my poore *Rosaline,* whether wilt thou goe?
Wilt thou change Fathers? I will giue thee mine: *95*
I charge thee be not thou more grieu'd then I am.
ROS. I haue more cause.
CEL. Thou hast not Cosen,
Prethee be cheereful; know'st thou not the Duke
Hath banish'd me his daughter?   *100*
ROS. That he hath not.
CEL. No, hath not? Rosaline lacks then the loue
Which teacheth thee that thou and I am one,
Shall we be sundred? shall we part sweete girle?
No, let my Father seeke another heire: *105*
Therefore deuise with me how we may flie
Whether to goe, and what to beare with vs,
And doe not seeke to take your change vpon you,
To beare your griefes your selfe, and leaue me out:
For by this heauen, now at our sorrowes pale;   *110*
Say what thou canst, Ile goe along with thee.

QUESTIONS

1. Write the forms for the plural of these MnE nouns: 'cat,' 'dog,' 'brush,' 'ox,' 'deer.' Make a list of all the plural nouns in this text. Is the practise for forming the plural in EMnE more like that of ME or that of MnE?

2. What is the practise here for forming the genitive case?

3. List all the verbal constructions. Is *do* used as it is in MnE? Are questions and negatives formed as they are in MnE? Is the spelling of the verbal constructions consistent? (The EMnE form of MnE 'banished' occurs in ll. 64, 87, and 100. Which probably best represents the actual pronunciation?) Does 'to' occur as the sign of the infinitive? How is the apostrophe used? All in all, do Shakespeare's verbal constructions seem to be closer to ME practise or to MnE practise?

4. What do you observe about the grammatical property of *concord* in l. 61? Are there other instances of this kind?

EXERCISE 10
ROMEO AND JULIET
I. i. 35–71, Shakespeare, 1623 Folio

SAMP.   Me they shall feele while I am able to stand: *35*
    And 'tis knowne I am a pretty peece of flesh.
GREG.   'Tis well thou art not Fish: If thou hadst thou
    had'st beene poore Iohn. Draw thy Toole,
    here comes (two) of the House of the *Mountagues.*

Enter two other Seruingmen.

SAM.   My naked weapon is out: quarrel, I will back thee.   *40*
GRE.   How? Turne thy backe, and run.
SAM.   Feare me not.
GRE.   No marry: I feare thee.
SAM.   Let vs take the Law of our sides: let them begin.
GRE.   I wil frown as I passe by, & let the(m) take it as they list.   *45*
SAM.   Nay, as they dare. I wil bite my Thumb at them,
    which is a disgrace to them, if they beare it.
ABRA.   Do you bite your Thumbe at vs sir?
SAMP.   I do bite my Thumbe, sir.
ABRA.   Do you bite your Thumbe at vs, sir?   *50*
SAM.   Is the law of our side, if I say I?   GRE. No.
SAM.   No sir, I do not bite my Thumbe at you sir: but
    I bite my Thumbe sir.
GREG.   Do you quarrell sir?
ABRA.   Quarrell sir? no sir.   *55*
SAM.   If you do sir, I am for you, I serue as good a man as you.
ABRA.   No better?   SAMP.   Well sir.

Enter Benuolio.

GR.   Say better: here comes one of my masters kinsmen.
SAMP.   Yes, better.
ABRA.   You Lye.   *60*
SAMP.   Draw if you be men.   GREGORY,   remember thy
    (s)washing blow.   *They fight.*
BEN.   Part Fooles, put vp your swords, you know not
    what you do.

Enter Tibalt.

TYB.   What are thou drawne, among these heartlesse   *65*
    Hindes? Turne thee Benuolio, looke vpon thy death.
BEN.   I do but keepe the peace, put vp thy Sword,
    Or manage it to part these men with me.

Reprinted from Albert H. Marckwardt, *Introduction to the English Language* (New York: Oxford University Press, 1942), by permission of the publisher.

TYB.   What draw, and talke of peace? I hate the word
      As I hate hell, all *Mountagues,* and thee: *70*
      Haue at thee Coward.   *Fight.*

QUESTIONS

In answering these questions use the texts for both Exercise 9 and Exercise 10.

1. List all the pronouns. In general, is the practise here similar to that of MnE? What are the forms of genitive pronouns? Under what circumstances are *my* and *mine* used? What is the practise for forming reflexive pronouns?

2. Observe the context in which the second person pronouns are used. When are the *y*-forms (*you,* etc.) used and when are the *th*-forms (*thou,* etc.) used? Prepare a general statement about Shakespeare's practise in maintaining a distinction between these two forms of the second person pronoun. Do you think MnE has gained or lost in its practise in this regard?

3. Read further in any edition of Shakespeare and in the Bible (Authorized Version, 1611) for examples of EMnE use of *it.* How does the practise here compare with MnE usage? Do you find any occurrence of the MnE practise exemplified in these two sentences:

    a. *It* rained yesterday.

    b. I found out that my car had lost *its* shine.

Consult the *OED* for its treatment of 'its.'

4. Are there any occurrences of prepositions which contrast with MnE usage? (In the text for Exercise 9, what do you make of l. 89?)

5. Is Shakespeare's use of adjectives and adverbs similar to MnE usage? (Extend your examination beyond the limit of these two texts; consider, too, the occurrence of comparative and superlative forms.)

EXERCISE 11
HAMLET
III. i. 1–92, Shakespeare, first printed 1603

A hall in the castle.
Enter HAMLET *and two or three of the*
PLAYERS.

HAMLET.

Speak the speech, I pray you, as I pronounced it to you, trippingly on the tongue;
but if you mouth it, as many of your players do, I
had as lief the town-crier spoke my lines. Nor do
not saw the air too much with your hand, thus;   5
but use all gently: for in the very torrent, tempest,
and, as I may say, the whirlwind of passion, you
must acquire and beget a temperance that may
give it smoothness. O, it offends me to the soul to
hear a robostious periwig-pated fellow tear a   10
passion to tatters, to very rags, to split the ears of
the groundlings, who, for the most part, are
capable of nothing but inexplicable dumb-shows
and noise: I would have such a fellow whipt for
o'erdoing Termagant; it out-herods Herod: pray   15
you, avoid it.

FIRST PLAYER.

I warrant your honour.

HAMLET.

But not too tame neither, but let your own dis-
cretion be your tutor: suit the action to the word,
the word to the action; with this special observ-   20
ance, that you o'erstep not the modesty of nature:
for anything so overdone is from the purpose of
playing, whose end, both at the first and now,
was and is, to hold, as 'twere, the mirror up to
nature; to show virtue her own feature, scorn her   25
own image, and the very age and body of the time
his form and pressure. Now, this overdone, or

Reprinted from *Hamlet*, Shakespeare Head Press Edition (New York: Oxford University Press).

come tardy off, though it make the unskilful
laugh, cannot but make the judicious grieve; the
censure of the which one must, in your allowance,   *30*
o'erweigh a whole theatre of others. O there be
players that I have seen play,—and heard others
praise, and that highly,—not to speak it pro-
fanely, that, neither having the accent of Chris-
tians, nor the gait of Christian, pagan, nor man,   *35*
have so strutted and bellowed, that I have thought
some of nature's journeymen had made them,
and not made them well, they imitated humanity
so abominably.

FIRST PLAYER.

I hope we have reform'd that indifferently with   *40*
us, sir.

HAMLET.

O, reform it altogether. And let those that play
your clowns speak no more than is set down for
them: for there be of them that will themselves
laugh, to set on some quantity of barren specta-   *45*
tors to laugh too; though, in the mean time, some
necessary question of the play be then to be consider'd; that's villainous, and shows a most pitiful
ambition in the fool that uses it. Go, make you
ready.   [*Exeunt* PLAYERS. *50*

Enter POLONIUS, ROSENCRANTZ, *and*
GUILDENSTERN.

How now, my lord! will the king hear this piece
of work?

POLONIUS.

And the queen, too, and that presently.

HAMLET.

Bid the players make haste.   [*Exeunt* POLONIUS.
Will you two help to hasten them?   *55*

ROSENCRANTZ *and* GUILDENSTERN.

We will, my lord.
                    [*Exeunt* ROSENCRANTZ *and* GUILDENSTERN.

HAMLET.

What, ho, Horatio!

Enter HORATIO.

HORATIO.

Here, sweet lord, at your service.

HAMLET.

Horatio, thou art e'en as just a man
As e'er my conversation coped withal. 60

HORATIO.

O, my dear lord, —

HAMLET.

     Nay, do not think I flatter;
For what advancement may I hope from thee,
That no revenue hast, but thy good spirits,
To feed and clothe thee? Why should the poor be flatter'd?
No, let the candied tongue lick absurd pomp; 65
And crook the pregnant hinges of the knee
Where thrift may follow fawning. Dost thou hear?
Since my dear soul was mistress of her choice,
And could of men distinguish, her election
Hath seal'd thee for herself: for thou hast been 70
As one, in suffering all, that suffers nothing;
A man that fortune's buffets and rewards
Hast ta'en with equal thanks: and blest are those
Whose blood and judgement are so well commingled,
That they are not a pipe for fortune's finger 75
To sound what stop she please. Give me that man
That is not passion's slave, and I will wear him
In my heart's core, ay, in my heart of heart,
As I do thee. — Something too much of this. —
There is a play to-night before the king; 80
One scene of it comes near the circumstance
Which I have told thee of my father's death:
I prithee, when thou seest that act a-foot,
Even with the very comment of thy soul
Observe my uncle: if his occulted guilt 85
Do not itself unkennel in one speech,
It is a damned ghost that we have seen;
And my imaginations are as foul
As Vulcan's stithy. Give him heedful note:
For I mine eyes will rivet to his face; 90
And, after, we will both our judgements join
In censure of his seeming.

QUESTION

Rewrite the prose section of this text as you would speak it in your normal conversation. Do the same thing for the first twenty lines of *As You Like It,* I. i. Do not fuss too much about changing Shakespeare's vocabulary (but by all means notice the difference between his and yours). Give first attention to syntactical changes. What modifications (word order, function words, etc.) did you have to make? Compare Shakespeare's prose with OE and ME prose. What changes must still occur before English prose becomes modern?

✠ ✠ ✠

TRANSITION

Although most of the significant linguistic features of Modern English are present, fixed in the language of 1700, by no means can we conclude that all writers from that time forward display a style and set of language habits which are totally similar to the average usage represented in contemporary English. To suggest the nature of language change still possible, and, what is more, to invite a consideration of the stability of grammatical features and the flexibility of rhetoric—to suggest, that is, that one should ask if the language is changing or if it is only the habits of usage, of style, which are changing—we have included two passages produced after 1600, one dated roughly at 1700, the other at 1800. These are the texts:

12. *The Battle of Dunbar*. Gilbert Burnet, d. 1715.
13. *A Defence of Poetry*. Percy Bysshe Shelley, d. 1822.

THE BATTLE OF DUNBAR
Gilbert Burnet, Bishop of Salisbury (d. 1715)
lines 1–37

The army was indeed one of the best that ever *Scotland* had brought together, but it was ill commanded: for all that had made defection from their cause, or that were thought indifferent as to either side, which they called detestable neutrality, were put out of commission. The preachers thought it an army of saints, and seemed well assured of success. They drew near *Cromwell,* who being   *5* pressed by them retired towards *Dunbar,* where his ships and provisions lay. The *Scots* followed him, and were posted on a hill about a mile from thence, where there was no attacking them. *Cromwell* was then in great distress, and looked on himself as undone. There was no marching towards *Berwick,* the ground was too narrow: Nor could he come back into the country without   *10* being separated from his ships, and starving his army. The least evil seemed to be to kill his horses, and put his army on board, and sail back to *Newcastle*; which, in the disposition that *England* was in at that time, would have been all their destruction, for it would have occasioned an universal insurrection for the King. They had not above three days' forage for their horses. So *Cromwell*   *15* called his officers to a day of seeking the Lord, in their style. He loved to talk much of that matter all his life long afterwards: He said he felt such an enlargement of heart in prayer, and such quiet upon it, that he bade all about him take heart, for God had certainly heard them, and would appear for them. After prayer they walked in the Earl of Roxburgh's gardens, that lie under the hill: *20* And by prospective glasses they discerned a great motion in the *Scotish* Camp: upon which *Cromwell* said, 'God is delivering them into our hands, they are coming down to us.' *Leslie* was in the chief command: but he had a committee of the States with him to give him his orders, among whom *Warriston* was one. These were weary of lying in the fields, and thought that *Leslie* made not haste   *25* enough to destroy those Sectaries; for so they loved to call them. He told them, by lying there all was sure, but that by engaging into action with gallant and desperate men all might be lost: Yet they still called on him to fall on. Many have thought that all this was treachery, done on design to deliver up our army to *Cromwell*; some laying it upon *Leslie,* and others upon my uncle. I am   *30* persuaded there was no treachery in it: only *Warriston* was too hot and *Leslie* was too cold, and yielded too easily to their humours, which he ought not to have done. They were all night employed in coming down the hill: And in the morning, before they were put in order, *Cromwell* fell upon them. Two regiments stood their ground, and were almost all killed in their ranks: The rest did run   *35* in a most shameful manner: So that both their artillery and baggage, and with these a great many prisoners, were taken, some thousands in all.

Reprinted from *The Oxford Book of English Prose,* edited by Sir Arthur Thomas Quiller-Couch (New York: The Oxford University Press, 1925).

QUESTIONS

This text, like that for Exercise 13, is a modern edition. Both texts will show, however, the general condition of English within two centuries of Shakespeare's death.

1. Are there any instances here of punctuation usage which does not yet quite accord with contemporary usage?

2. Can you, from observation of the punctuation, come to any conclusion about sentence rhythm? Do these sentences sound like contemporary sentences?

3. If you were to rewrite this passage, would you feel obliged to make any changes in vocabulary or structure? Is *do* used the same way you would use it?

4. If there were no date for this text, and you were to find it, would you regard it as 'fairly recent,' 'old fashioned,' good or bad writing? Why?

A DEFENCE OF POETRY
Percy Bysshe Shelley (d. 1822)
lines 1–51

Poetry is indeed something divine. It is at once the centre and circumference
of knowledge; it is that which comprehends all science, and that to which all
science must be referred. It is at the same time the root and blossom of all other
systems of thought; it is that from which all spring, and that which adorns all;
and that which, if blighted, denies the fruit and seed, and withholds from the   5
barren world the nourishment and the succession of the scions of the tree of
life. It is the perfect and consummate surface and bloom of all things; it is as the
odour and the colour of the rose to the texture of the elements which compose
it, as the form and splendour of unfaded beauty to the secrets of anatomy and
corruption. What were virtue, love, patriotism, friendship—what were the   10
scenery of this beautiful universe which we inhabit; what were our consolations
on this side of the grave—and what were our aspirations beyond it, if poetry
did not ascend to bring light and fire from those eternal regions where the owl-
winged faculty of calculation dare not ever soar? Poetry is not like reasoning,
a power to be exerted according to the determination of the will. A man cannot   15
say, 'I will compose poetry.' The greatest poet even cannot say it; for the mind
in creation is as a fading coal, which some invisible influence, like an inconstant
wind, awakens to transitory brightness; this power arises from within, like the
colour of a flower which fades and changes as it is developed, and the conscious
portions of our natures are unprophetic either of its approach or its departure.   20
Could this influence be durable in its original purity and force, it is impossible
to predict the greatness of the results; but when composition begins, inspiration
is already on the decline, and the most glorious poetry that has ever been
communicated to the world is probably a feeble shadow of the original con-
ceptions of the poet.   25

Poetry is the record of the best and happiest moments of the happiest and
best minds. We are aware of evanescent visitations of thought and feeling
sometimes associated with place or person, sometimes regarding our own mind
alone, and always arising unforeseen and departing unbidden, but elevating
and delightful beyond all expression: so that even in the desire and regret they   30
leave, there cannot but be pleasure, participating as it does in the nature of its
object. It is as it were the interpenetration of a diviner nature through our
own; but its footsteps are like those of a wind over the sea, which the coming
calm erases, and whose traces remain only, as on the wrinkled sand which paves
it. These and corresponding conditions of being are experienced principally by   35
those of the most delicate sensibility and the most enlarged imagination; and
the state of mind produced by them is at war with every base desire. The

Reprinted from *The Oxford Book of English Prose*, edited by Sir Arthur Thomas Quiller-Couch
(New York: University of Oxford Press), by permission of The Clarendon Press.

enthusiasm of virtue, love, patriotism, and friendship, is essentially linked with such emotions; and whilst they last, self appears as what it is, an atom to a universe. Poets are not only subject to these experiences as spirits of the most refined organization, but they can colour all that they combine with the evanescent hues of this ethereal world; a word, a trait in the representation of a scene or a passion, will touch the enchanted chord, and reanimate, in those who have ever experienced these emotions, the sleeping, the cold, the buried image of the past. Poetry thus makes immortal all that is best and most beautiful in the world; it arrests the vanishing apparitions which haunt the interlunations of life, and veiling them, or in language or in form, sends them forth among mankind, bearing sweet news of kindred joy to those with whom their sisters abide—abide, because there is no portal of expression from the caverns of the spirit which they inhabit into the universe of things. Poetry redeems from decay the visitations of the divinity in man. *40* *45* *50*

QUESTIONS

By the beginning of the nineteenth century the grammatical features of English have, for the most part, assumed the look and sound of contemporary English. This passage presents no structural difficulties to the contemporary reader.

1. Would you call it, however, ordinary, contemporary English?
2. What would you say about its diction (vocabulary)?
3. What would you say about its style—formal, stilted, concise, what? How would you rate it, good or bad?
4. Consult other first editions of early nineteenth-century English prose, both American and British, and prepare a paper describing what you feel to be the principal differences between early nineteenth-century and twentieth-century English.

✠ ✠ ✠

PHONOLOGICAL
AND SEMANTIC CHANGE

Change in language is not confined to structural evolution. Just as the syntax of English has changed over the centuries, so too have its sounds and vocabulary changed. As a matter of fact, changes in sound and changes in word meanings are often more dramatic than structural changes. To illustrate these developments in English we have included these two exercises:

14. *Phonological Change:* a series of questions is given to demonstrate how the quality of English phonemes has changed from the Old English period to the present time.

15. *Semantic Change:* a series of questions is given to demonstrate how the meaning of a word can change over the course of centuries; four classes of change are illustrated—specialization, generalization, pejoration, and amelioration.

PHONOLOGICAL CHANGE

If you have heard either Chaucer's poetry or Old English poetry read aloud you know that the sounds you heard are not those of Modern English. OE poetry sounded something more like German and Chaucer's poetry at least like a foreign language. Shakespeare's poetry too, read properly, would sound different, not quite so strange as Chaucer's language, but certainly not like our language. Our ear provides evidence of phonological change. Before setting out on a discussion of the history of English sounds, however, we will begin by stating very briefly the kinds of testimony we possess which demonstrate that the sounds of English have changed. A few sounds have been lost, as we shall see, and the stressed vowels and diphthongs in many words which were present in OE have changed their quality. How do scholars know what English sounded like centuries ago? There are four types of evidence which have proved extremely valuable.

First, the spelling displayed in the text being examined, particularly unorthodox or uneducated forms, is often a clear hint about how a word was pronounced. Suppose, for example, a contemporary writer from the northeastern United States were to spell *cah baan,* instead of 'car barn'; we would be correct in assuming that his spelling reflected actual pronunciation more accurately than conventional spelling does. Second, some writers were contemporary observers of language, and they have left us their comments about various pronunciations and peculiarities of usage. You have read (Exercise 8) what Higden and John of Trevisa thought about certain fourteenth-century pronunciations. In the sixteenth century Sir Thomas Elyot complained about some 'corrupt and foul' pronunciations certain young men had learned from their 'nurses and other foolish women.' Observations of that sort indicate that not all speakers sounded alike, and that some speakers disapproved of the speech of others, probably indicating their own conservative reaction to change. Third, the evidence of rhymes, puns, or other plays on words is highly reliable information about pronunciation. When Chaucer rhymes *heeth* (MnE 'heath') with *breeth* (MnE 'breath') where we cannot rhyme 'heath' with 'breath,' we can conclude that one of the pronunciations has changed. Similarly, Pope's famed couplet from *The Rape of the Lock,*

> Here thou, great Anna! whom three realms obey,
> Dost sometimes counsel take—and sometimes tea

confirms the pronunciation of some of your great-grandmothers—*obey* has not changed, therefore *tea* was pronounced as if, today, it rhymed with 'say,' not with 'see.' Fourth, some dialectal pronunciations preserve earlier standard pronunciations. The odd spelling *jine* for 'join' suggests the earlier standard pronunciation; instead of rhyming with contemporary 'loin' it must have rhymed with 'line.' Philologists, working with massive data and accumulating evidence from these four types of information, and from other sources too, have, with fair to remarkable success, been able to reconstruct the sounds of English in their earlier stages of development. Sometimes the changes have been thoroughly regular. For example, every word which Shakespeare would have pronounced with the diphthong used in MnE 'main' is today pronounced with the diphthong used in MnE 'mean.' Such regularity suggests a phonological law. Not all the changes which have occurred are that orderly, although, when you have seen more evidence, you will be able to conclude that the directions of phonological change have not been altogether arbitrary and that some of them can be explained quite reasonably.

Because thorough competence in phonology (the study of the sounds employed in a language) requires a great deal of work—and lies beyond the scope of this exercise—you will observe here a set of restricted texts. Therefore not every phonological change which has occurred in English can be demonstrated, although the principal ones will be. We must start by considering the need for a neutral alphabet to represent the sounds of English. Conventional spelling, although more so now than it used to be, is not altogether logical or consistent. We use the same set of spelling characters to represent more than one sound. For example, the actual value (sound) of the stressed diphthong in 'say' is identical with that of 'weigh,' 'main,' and 'pale'; 'ay,' 'ei,' 'ai,' and 'a–e' all represent the same sound. A careful analysis of the relationship between sound and spelling will reveal many more examples of mismatching of sound and spelling. The problem arises because our alphabet of twenty-six characters is used to represent at least thirty-one to thirty-three sounds, the actual sounds used in contemporary English. A phonemic notation, using one character to represent only one sound, will suit our present need. We say, when we use such a system, that we transcribe speech, or a written text, into phonemic notation, or that we make a phonemic transcription. Awareness of the distinction between a phonetic and a phonemic transcription is not important for this exercise. Neither will it be necessary to annotate stress, pitch, or juncture. For the purpose of this exercise we will establish these guides:

a. a phoneme is a set of sounds, so restricted that a single sound must belong to only *one* set; no sound can belong to more than one set; therefore, the sets are mutually exclusive and contrast with each other, e.g., of 'see' and 'say' we can state that the initial consonant of both belongs to the same set, but the stressed diphthongs of each belong to different sets

b. the following equivalencies are established between the symbol used and the sound it represents:

Consonants

b	*b*ait	s	*s*in
d	*d*ate	š	*sh*in
f	*f*ate	t	*t*in
g	*g*ate	θ	*th*igh
k	*c*ake	ð	*th*y
h	*h*ate	v	*v*an
m	*m*ate	z	*z*est
n	*n*o	ž	vi*s*ion, *Zh*ivago
ŋ	sa*ng*	č	*ch*urch
p	*p*ark	ǰ	*j*oke, Geor*g*e

Semi-Vowels

l	*l*ay
r	*r*ay
y	*y*ell
w	*w*ay

Vowels

	FRONT	CENTRAL	BACK
High	i b<u>i</u>t	ɨ start<u>e</u>d	u b<u>oo</u>k
Mid	e b<u>e</u>t	ə b<u>u</u>t	ɔ b<u>ou</u>ght
Low	æ b<u>a</u>t	a b<u>o</u>x	

The vowels are placed in this chart, labelled as indicated, to show the relative point of articulation of the vowel. Think of the left as close to the lips of the mouth, the right side as close to the back of the mouth, the top close to the roof of the mouth, and the bottom as lower down. The tongue mass moves into approximately one of the nine available positions when the vowel is uttered. Front vowels are articulated with the lips unrounded, back vowels with the lips rounded. The jaw also drops lower as the vowel uttered is lower. (Why does the physician ask you to utter /a/ when he wishes to examine your throat?)

Diphthongs (combine a vowel with a semi-vowel)

Those diphthongs made with a vowel and the semi-vowel /y/ are articulated closer to the front of the mouth than the ones made with the semi-vowel /w/ are.

iy	b*ea*t	uw	b*oo*t
ey	b*ai*t	ow	b*oa*t
oy	b*oy*	aw	(a)b*ou*t
ay	b*i*te		

We will add two other combinations of sound:
yuw, 'be*auty*,' to distinguish a transcription of that combination of sounds from the sound of the stressed diphthong in 'boot.' It is also the difference between 'feud' and 'food.'
-ər, the sound of the last syllable in 'sing*er*.'
Some sample phonemic transcriptions, using the equivalencies from the table, follow; study them and then transcribe the words and passages listed below. Remember, transcription represents sounds, as used in normal conversation, *not* spellings. Transcriptions are placed within slant lines: /—/.

packed /pækt/   sink /siŋk/   food /fuwd/
rise /rayz/   mother /məðər/   feud /fyuwd/
rice /rays/   table /teybəl/   witty /witiy/
vision /vižən/   floor /flɔr/   believe /bəliyv/
elevator /eləveytər/   singer /siŋər/   baited /beytid/
shining /šayniŋ/   finger /fiŋgər/   shop /šap/
hangar /hæŋər/   church /čərč/   shopped /šapt/
hunger /həŋgər/   Charlie /čarliy/   jabbed /jæbd/
Friday and Saturday afternoon /fraydiy ən sætərdiy æftərnuwn/
I'll take sugar and spice /ayl teyk šugər ən spays/

TRANSCRIBE

1. Sunday, Monday, and Tuesday
2. April, May, June, and July
3. see saw Marjorie Daw
4. Sue sells sea shells
5. Four score and twenty years ago our forefathers brought forth upon this nation
6. application
7. penny
8. pen knife
9. weigh
10. wail
11. whale
12. who's in a hurry
13. where's the fire
14. pumpkin pie and ice cream
15. cheese and crackers got all muddy

So far in this exercise we have conducted a preliminary discussion necessary for a consideration of historical phonological change. We may now move to that consideration. Printed below are three short passages. Those in OE and ME you have already seen in earlier exercises. But you will notice that the passage in OE, the opening lines, once again, of "The Legend of St. Andrew," does not correspond precisely with the same lines as they are printed in Exercise 1. Here the text has been normalized and altered to fit the orthographical practise current in the Late West Saxon dialect. There are several reasons for using now a normalized text. You can, to begin with, compare the two versions to see how the spellings differ, and that type of experience in making a contrastive analysis should provide for you an insight into a technique which has proved most useful to the historical linguist, although, to be quite honest, the texts are too short to enable you to make more than a superficial analysis. More important, using the Late West Saxon dialect assures us of tracing the development of sound changes from the widest base of OE—most of the OE documents are preserved in this dialect. Should you continue your study of OE you would discover the importance, in the development of English, of other OE dialects. For the present it is sufficient to restrict the data to the evidence of this one dialect.

Accompanying each passage is a transcription employing the notation you have just learned. Where sounds occur (and are transcribed) which are different from sounds found in MnE, they are explained. Study the passages carefully and read the transcriptions aloud. It is a good idea to read each aloud as many times as you need to until you feel you can read each passage easily, reproducing, as the transcription indicates, the sounds (so far as we are able to reconstruct them) which would have been heard at the time the original was produced. Then answer the questions which follow. The same passages which you have already studied in OE and ME are used here again because, to complete this exercise, you need to know the MnE equivalent of the words in the text; there are no unfamiliar words in the EMnE text.

I. OE

Hēr sæġþ þæt *æfter* þām þe Drihten Hǣlend *Crist* tō heo-
heyr sæyθ θæt æfter θa:m θe drixten hæ:lend kriy:st tow: heo

fenum āstāh, *þæt* þā apostoli *wǣron* ætsomne. And hīe *sendon*
vənum a:sta:x θæt θa: apəstəliy wæ:rɔn ætsɔmne and hiy:ə sendɔn

hlot him betwēonum,   hwider hira ġehwelċ faran *sceolde*   *tō*
hlɔt him betwey:ownum hwider hira yehwelċ faran šeowlde tow:

lǣrenne. Sæ̆ġþ þæt sē   ēadiga Matheus ġehlēat *tō*   Marmadonia
læ:ren:e sæyθ θæt sey: æ:ədigə maθeus yehlæ:ət tow: marmədowniə

þǣre ċeastre. Sæ̆ġþ þonne *þæt* þā *men* þe on þǣre ċeastre   5
θæ:rə čæəstre sæyθ θon:e θæt θa: men θe ɔn θæ:rə čæəstre

wēron, þæt hīe   *hlāf* ne ǣton, nē   *wæter* ne *druncon;* ac hīe
wæ:rɔn θæt hiy:ə xla:f ne æ:tɔn ney: wæter ne drunkɔn ak hiy:ə

ǣton manna līċhaman and hiera *blōd*   *druncon.* And ǣ̆ġhwelċ
æ:tɔn man:a liy:čaman and hiəra blow:d drunkɔn and æ:yhwelċ

man þe on þǣre ċeastre cōm   elþēodisc,   sæ̆ġþ þæt hīe   *hīne sūnu*
man θe ɔn θæ:re čæəstre kow:m elθey:owdiš sæyθ θæt hiy:ə hine sow:na

ġenōmon   and *his* ēagan *ūt* āstungon, and hīe   *him sealdon āttor*
yenow:man and his æ:əgan uw:t a:stungɔn and hiy:ə him sæəldɔn a:t:ɔr

drincan þæt mid miclum lybcræfte *wæs ġeblanden,* and mid   10
drinkan θæt mid miklum lybkræfte wæs yeblanden and mid

þām þe hīe   þone *drenc druncon,* hraþe hiera heorte   *wæs* tōlīesed
θam θey hiy:ə θɔne drenč drunkɔn xraθe hiəra heowrte wæs tow:liy:əsed

and hiere mōd   onwended.
and hiərə mow:d ɔnwended

NOTES

1. The notation /:/ after a character indicates that the sound is long; not different but longer; i.e., more time is consumed in saying it. It is very important to observe the short–long distinction.

2. The character /x/ represents the sound of the spelling *ch* in the German word *ach*.

3. The character /Y/ represents a high-front-rounded vowel which has the sound of the spelling *ü* in the German word *müssen*.

4. You will also need the words in the following list for this exercise:

OE Spelling	Transcription	MnE Spelling
nama	nama	name
sǣ	sæ:	sea
dæġ	dæy	day
healfe	hæəlfe	half
wē	wey:	we
crabba	krab:a	crab
ðynnum	θYn:um	thin
lǣdan	læ:dan	lead (v.)
yfele	Yfelə	evil
æcer	æker	acre

II. ME

Ther was also   a *Nonne*, a *Prioresse*,
θær   was alsow: ə nun   ə priy:ɔres:ə

That of *hir smyling*   was *ful   simple and coy;*
θat   ɔf ir smiy:ling was ful simpl   and koy

Hir gretteste *ooth*   was *but* by *seynte* Loy;
ir   gret:əst ɔ:θ   was but bi sæintə loy

And *she* was cleped   *madame* Eglentyne.
and šey: was kley:pəd madam egləntiy:nə

Ful wel she song the *service divyne*,   5
ful wel šey: sɔng θə servisə diviy:nə

Entuned   in hir *nose* ful *semely;*
entyuwnəd in ir   nɔ:z ful sey:məli

And Frensh she   spak ful faire and fetisly,
and frenš   šey: spak ful fæir and fetisli

After   the *scole*   of Stratford atte Bowe,
æftər θə   skow:l ɔf stratfɔrd at:ə bɔ:wə

For Frensh of Paris was *to*   *hir unknowe.*
fɔr frenš ɔf paris was tow: ir unknɔ:wə

At *mete   wel y-taught* was she *with-alle;*   10
at mæ:tə wel itawxt   was šey: wiθal:ə

She leet *no morsel* from hir *lippes* falle,
šey: ley:t nɔ: mɔrsəl frɔm ir lip:əs fal:ə

Ne *wette* hir *fingres* in hir *sauce depe.*
nə wet: ir fingrəs in ir   sawsə dey:pə

Wel coude she   carie a *morsel,* and *wel kepe,*
wel kuw,d šey: kari ə mɔrsəl and wel key:pə

That *no   drope* ne fille up-on hir *brest.*
θæt nɔ: drɔp nə fil: upɔn ir brest

In curteisye was *set* ful *muche* hir lest.   15
in kuwrtæisi was set ful mutš ir   lest

NOTES

1. You will need two more words for this exercise:

ME Spelling	*Transcription*	*MnE Spelling*
mous	muw:s	mouse
houndes	huw:ndəs	hounds

2. You will observe that the final -e occurring at the end of a line of verse has been transcribed /ə/, indicating that it was pronounced. In Exercise 5, however, the first line of this passage, which ends in a final -e, was scanned, and there it was suggested that the final -e at the end of the line of verse was *not* pronounced. The older view is that every final -e occurring at the end of a line of verse *was* pronounced. Today all authorities do not agree; there are some who believe that the rhythm of the line is the best guide in this matter, and that if the line does not *demand* it, to fit the basic iambic meter, it should not be pronounced. Unfortunately, we cannot reconstitute a fourteenth century Londoner to settle the issue.

III. EMnE

Oh that this too too solid Flesh, would melt,
ow: ðæt ðis tuw: tuw: sɔlid fleš wuw:ld melt

Thaw, and resolue it selfe into a Dew:
θɔ: ænd rizɔlv itself intuw: ə duw

Or that the Eurlasting had not fixt
ɔr ðæt ði evərlæstiŋ hæd nɔt fikst

His Cannon 'gainst Selfe-slaughter. O God, O God!
hiz kænən gæinst self slɔ:tr ow: gɔd ow: gɔd

How weary, stale, flat, and vnprofitable   5
həw wey:ri stæ:l flæt ənd unprɔfitæ:bl

Seemes to me all the vses of this world?
siy:mz tə miy: ɔ:l ðə yuwsiz əv ðis wɔrld

Fie on't? Oh fie, fic, 'tis an vnweeded Garden
fəy ɔnt ow: fəy fəy tiz ən unwiy:did gærdn

That growes to Seed: Things rank, and grosse in Nature
ðæt grow:z tə siy:d θiŋz ræŋk ənd grow:s in næ:tyər

Possesse it meerely. That it should come to this:
pəzes it miy:rli ðæt it šuw:ld kum tə ðis

But two monthes dead: Nay, not so much; not two,   10
but tuw: munθs ded næi nɔt sow: muč nɔt tuw:

So excellent a King, that was to this
sow: eksəlent ə kiŋ ðæt wæz tə ðis

Hiperion to a Satyre: so louing to my Mother
həypey:ryən tuw: a sæ:tir sow: luviŋ tə məy muðr

That he might not beteeme the windes of heauen
ðæt i məyt nɔt bitiy:m ðə windz əv hevn

Visit her face too roughly. Heauen and Earth
vizit ər fæ:s tuw: rufli hevn ənd erθ

Must I remember: why she would hang on him,   15
must əy rimembr wəy šiy wuw:ld hæŋ ɔn im

As if encrease of Appetite had growne
əz if inkrey:z   əv æpətəyt həd grow:n

By   what it fed on;
bəy wæt it fed ɔn

NOTES

Also use these words for this exercise:

EMnE Spelling	Transcription	MnE Spelling
teares	tey:rz	tears
reason	rey:zn	reason
toy	toy	toy
vnrighteous	unrəytyəs	unrighteous
doubt	dəwt	doubt

After you have read these passages and have made yourself familiar with the transcriptions, you are in a position to commence a preliminary investigation of the development of English sounds. But you do not have sufficient information to make a thorough study, because, for one thing, nothing has been indicated about the occurrence of stress (relative loudness in pronunciation) in the earlier stages of the language or how, in some instances, it shifted. But you can make a good many observations with the limited data you have. Begin by preparing charts, one for each transcription shown above. Draw sixteen columns on a piece of paper, one for each of the MnE stressed vowels and diphthongs displayed earlier in this exercise; omit the high central vowel /ɨ/ but add /ər/. Your chart, at the beginning, will look like this:

OE CHART

MnE	bit	bet	bat	but	box	book	bought
	i	e	æ	ə	a	u	ɔ
			æfter				

beat	bait	boy	bite	boot	boat	bout	– er	feud
iy	ey	oy	ay	uw	ow	zw	ər	yuw
			kriy:st	tow:				

Make three charts, one for OE, one for ME, and one for EMnE. For each transcription (and using all words from each list of transcriptions added after a text), place the *transcription* of each word which is italicized in the text (from the EMnE text place each word) in the column headed by the stressed vowel or diphthong which represents the contemporary pronunciation of its stressed vowel or diphthong. The three *italicized* words in the first line of the OE text would be placed on your OE chart as follows:

æfter (stressed vowel in OE is *æ*): in the *æ* column, because the stressed vowel in MnE 'after' is also *æ*; place /æfter/ there

Crist (stressed vowel in OE is *iy:*): in the *ay* column, because the stressed diphthong in MnE 'Christ' is *ay*; place /kriy:st/ there

tō (stressed vowel in OE is *ow:*): in the *uw* column, because the stressed diphthong in MnE 'to' is *uw*; place /tow:/ there

Complete these charts.

QUESTIONS

With the preceding charts as your evidence, answer the following questions.

1. What would have been the missing forms in this chart? The entries are transcriptions, not spellings.

OE	ME	MnE
nama	_____	neym
_____	giltes	gilts
sun:e	sun:ə	_____
muw:s	_____	maws
fey:dan	fey:d	_____
_____	stɔ:n	stown
man	_____	mæn
_____	koy	koy
sendan	sendə	_____
_____	riy:də	rayd

(Note: a shortcoming in the transcription system we have used shows up here. The fourth entry in the OE column (muw:s) accurately represents the OE spelling *mūs,* but the symbol used to represent the OE long vowel *ū* is a diphthong symbol. You must look to the *spellings* of the OE text to identify an OE diphthong. Double vowel spellings in OE are diphthongs. There are eight of them: ea, ēa; eo, ēo; io, īo; ie, īe. Therefore *ē* in OE is a long vowel, pronounced /ey:/; although we have to use the symbol of a MnE diphthong to represent it, *ē*, in OE, was a vowel. When you consider the development of the OE vowels and diphthongs, look to the OE spellings—the transcriptions represent their quality, or equivalent sound value.)

2. For this question we shall agree that MnE has seven vowels: /i, e, æ, ə, a, u, ɔ/.

  a. What OE vowels are not present in MnE?

  b. What MnE vowels were present in OE?

  c. Are there any MnE vowels not present in OE?

  d. Which OE vowels were most stable (i.e., exhibit the least change from OE to MnE)?

3. For this question we shall agree that MnE has seven diphthongs, (iy, ey, oy, ay, uw, ow, aw/, and the combinations /yuw, ər/.

  a. What are the OE sources of the MnE diphthongs?

  b. Are any unaccounted for by OE sources? If so, can you account for that fact?

4. Repeat questions 2 and 3 for ME.

5. In their transition from OE to ME were the vowels and dipthongs stable, very stable, or not very stable?

6. Repeat questions 2, 3, and 5 for EMnE.

7. Do you observe any instance, in any of the three stages, of a change in sound in a short vowel or diphthong where the same change did not occur in the long version of the same sound? ME *drope* (1. 14, p. 438) and ME *ooth* (1. 3, p. 438) became what MnE words? Are there other similar occurrences? Are the long or the short sounds the most stable?

8. With your response to question 7 in mind, can you formulate a statement about the ME *spellings* of vowels and diphthongs?

9. Sometime before the beginning of the ME period and ending sometime after the beginning of the EMnE period all the vowels of English went through a change which has been called 'The Great Vowel Shift.' Consult any of the textbooks which have been mentioned in these exercises for a description of that shift. Does the evidence which you have assembled here confirm the general description you read?

10. Are there any consonants in MnE which were not present in any of the three earlier stages of English?

11. Are there any consonants in any of the three earlier stages which are not present in MnE? If so, have they been replaced by other sounds? What has been the history of what in MnE we spell '-ing'? Consult the *OED* for earlier pronunciations of 'doubt,' 'dumb,' 'doom'; what do you find? What appears to be the source of the MnE spelling 'gh'?

12. What appears to be the effect of the occurrence of one of the semi-vowels next to a vowel?

13. Some consonant changes can be explained by observing the movements of the tongue as sounds are articulated (pronounced) and by knowing what changes a shift in stress can cause. For example, MnE 'feature' was at one time trisyllabic and was pronounced with heavy stress on the first and last syllables: /fíy ti ùr/. It lost its heavy final stress, changed its final vowel to /ə/, and became disyllabic: /fíy tiər/. It can be shown that /i/ before a lightly stressed vowel tends to become a semi-vowel: thus, /fíy tyər/. It can also be shown that the occurrence of /ty/ causes an assimilation to take place. The tongue positions for /t/ and /y/ are quite close, and in the movement from the first to the second it fell into the position for /č/: thus, /fíy čər/. See if

you now can explain how the MnE pronunciation of *nature* developed from the pronunciation of it indicated in 1. 8, p. 439.

14. Although a good deal has been skipped in this exercise, you are, nonetheless, in a position now to prepare a first paper, or class discussion, on the development of English sounds. Do that.

EXERCISE 15
SEMANTIC CHANGE

Just as the structure (and therefore the grammar) and the sounds of English have changed over the years of its history and use, so too has its vocabulary changed. We have observed already one manifestation of vocabulary change, the appearance of loan words in the language. Other changes also took place, resulting, in addition to gains in the word stock, to some losses, as words formerly in the lexicon of English have dropped out. The *OED,* for example, lists many forms which are labelled 'obsolete,' no longer in use. Perhaps more striking has been the fate of words, both native English words and loan words, during the centuries of their existence in our language. It can be stated with almost the authority of a general law that *not all* words retain, in general usage, the meanings which they originally had. A *deer* for Shakespeare was not what we would call a 'deer'; 'knave' would not have meant to Chaucer what it means to us; a 'nice girl' (for us) would have implied something quite different to Samuel Johnson: hundreds of examples could be cited to show that changes in meaning, often drastic, have occurred.

It is not always possible to demonstrate why these changes took place. Perhaps a simplified explanation of the *semantic process* will help to identify some of the difficulties involved in trying to account for changes in meaning. Linguistic Semantics (not to be confused with General Semantics, an altogether different matter) is the study of meaning. The semanticist regards what we call *word* as an arbitrary symbol, which, as is true of all symbols, has no (contains no) meaning in itself, but points to, or stands for, something outside of itself where meaning may be said to reside. From this diagram we infer that an *observer* (or communicator) perceives a *sign* (symbol or word), follows its signal (direction) to an area of the *referent* (all contextual experience), selects the *meaning* equivalent (corresponding) to the *sign* for that contextual situation, and receives *comprehension.* Thus in each linguistic community speakers have agreed upon a large number of arbitrary signs as carriers

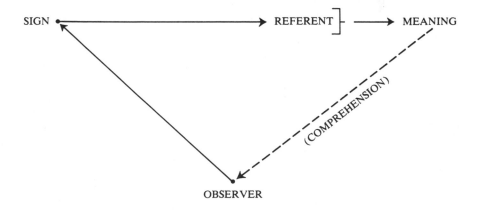

(when combined into the *code* by structural signals) of their *messages*. It is possible that conditions conducive to change may exist at any of the five stages represented in the diagram. The sign may change in form, the referent may narrow or enlarge, meaning may add or substract elements, comprehension may shift, and the attitude of the observer, towards all four of the other stages, may change. In actual usage, over the centuries, any or all of those forces may exert pressures on "word meanings" as the speakers of the language, constantly mobile in social situations, engage in the process of communication. When we do inquire into meaning, however, at least three other conditions, semantic environments, must be accounted for:

1. *Regional Variants.* A 'pail' to one speaker of English is a 'bucket' to another speaker. A 'dope' in one region is a 'coke' or 'coca-cola' in another, and may at the same time in both regions be a "dull, foolish person."

2. *Context.* If we ask for a 'pipe' in one store we will not receive the same object someone else will receive when he asks for a pipe in a different store.

3. *Time.* In the eighteenth century, when one traveled, he might have ridden in a 'coach.' If he traveled in the nineteenth century, the coach he rode in would have been quite different from the vehicle used by the traveler a century before, although called the same. And the twentieth century traveler, going 'coach fare,' could ride in a bus, a train, or an airplane.

Why do words change their meanings, and what must be considered when meaning is investigated are, as it should now be clear, vexing questions. It is much easier to observe *what* has happened.

Words change their meanings in one of four ways. They may generalize, specialize, pejorate, or ameliorate. An example of each type of change is illustrated by the development of the meaning of 'dedicate,' 'wife,' 'churl,' and 'steward.' Consult the *OED* for the history of the meanings attached, at different times, to those words. In general, this is what you will find:

1. 'Dedicate' has *generalized*. At first it was restricted in usage to indicating that one offered his person, service, or work to God. Now one may dedicate his person, service, or work to anyone or anything, and buildings or memorials can be dedicated. Obviously the area of the referent has enlarged. Note, too, that all the earlier meanings are still in general use.

2. 'Wife' has *specialized*. At first a wife was any adult female, but now she is a married female. In time, 'woman' took over the earlier meaning of wife. Obviously the area of the referent has restricted. Note that the earlier meaning is *not* now in general use.

3. 'Churl' has *pejorated*. At first 'churl' meant any country fellow, a rustic, but now the implication of unsavory moral behaviour is attached to it. In 900 "a good churl" was a permitted utterance; today, unless used ironically, it would not be understood. Obviously the attitude taken by speakers towards the referent has changed. The earlier meaning is no longer in general use.

4. 'Steward' has *ameliorated*. At first a keeper or guardian of a hall or sty (perhaps a pig sty), a steward now may be a respected public official or officer of a club. Its development has been just the opposite of that of 'churl.' The earlier meaning has been obscured.

It is convenient to divide these four types of semantic change into two sets of two changes, to show further the permissible changes a word may experience.

REFERENTIAL CHANGES   ATTITUDE CHANGES
(*Denotation*)   (*Connotation*)
Generalization   Pejoration
Specialization   Amelioration

At the same time, change is permitted in the direction of one member of each set and one member of the other set. Thus, a word cannot, for example, generalize and specialize at the same time, nor can it pejorate and ameliorate at the same time, but it could generalize and pejorate, or generalize and ameliorate, or specialize and pejorate, or specialize and ameliorate at the same time. And some words, having taken one direction, have, at a later time, reversed that direction.

QUESTIONS

1. Consult the *OED* to discover the semantic development of each word in the following list. In each instance, state

    a. what type of semantic change is illustrated
    b. whether the older meanings still survive in contemporary usage
    c. what periods of over-lapping of meanings occurred, if any
    d. what word has replaced it, if it did not survive

article	disease	lewd	pretty
bard	drive	libel	proposition
butcher	enthusiasm	lust	ring (n.)
chest	flesh	marshall	sail (v.)
chivalry	fond	martyr	smirk
circumstance	governor	meat	starve
coast (n.)	harlot	nice	thing
corn	hussy	pen	undertaker
counterfeiter	injury	picture	villain
crafty	knight	pirate	virtue

    2. Do semantic changes appear to occur more readily in words belonging to one part of speech class than to words in another class?
    3. Do loan words appear to be subjected to change to the same degree as native English words?

AN ADDED NOTE

Some attention to word borrowing and semantic change is an antidote to the 'etymological fallacy.' Etymology, as you have now determined, is not always a safe guide for determining the *present* meaning of a word. A distinguished American poet once deplored such phrases as 'Crime Crusade' and 'Cancer Crusade' because he believed 'crusade' should be restricted to mean the activities of religiously motivated men in the Middle Ages who 'took up the cross' to defend Christianity against attacks by 'heathens.' Not only did he ignore the historical fact that those medieval gentlemen had to travel thousands of miles from their homes to wage that defense, committing quite as many atrocities along the way as performing noble deeds, but he also failed to comprehend that 'Crime Crusade' and 'Cancer Crusade' are utterly sanctioned by contemporary usage. One might not like to hear 'crusade' used in that way, but it is useless to deplore, and not particularly honest to suggest to others, that it is wrong, or in bad taste, to use it that way.

It may not be unnecessary to add, also, that this one exercise does not exhaust the subject of semantic change. Still to be investigated would be such phenomena as euphemism, genteelism, hyperbole, understatement (litotes), folk-etymology, slang, British-American differences in usage, word coinage, and ironic use of language. All are interesting topics. This has been a restricted exercise. Additional information about semantic change and loan words, moreover, may prove rewarding Seek it in these two excellent books:

1. Mary S. Serjeanston. *A History of Foreign Words in English*. New York: Dutton, 1936.

2. Gustav Stern. *Meaning and Change of Meaning*. Gothenburg: Wettergren and Kerber, 1931.

✠ ✠ ✠

SUMMARY

Two sets of parallel passages have been placed at the end of these exercises to provide data for a discussion of the development of English from its earliest period to the present time. These are the texts:

16. *De Consolatione Philosophiæ,* Boethius
    a. the Latin text, 524
    b. Alfred's translation, 900
    c. Chaucer's translation, 1400
    d. the translation of Queen Elizabeth I, 1593
    e. a modern translation, 1962

17. *The New Testament,* Matthew vi. 9–21
    a. Gothic Text, 360
    b. Old English Text, 1000
    c. Middle English, Wycliffe, 1389
    d. Early Modern English, Tyndale, 1526
    e. Modern English, Monsignor Knox, 1944
    f. Modern English, Revised Standard Version, 1952

EXERCISE 16
PARALLEL TEXTS OF
DE CONSOLATIONE PHILOSOPHIÆ
III, vii, 1–58

The Latin Text
BOETHIUS,
524

Felix qui potuit boni
Fontem uisere lucidum,
Felix qui potuit grauis
Terræ soluere uincula.
Quondam funera coniugis   5
Vates threicius gemens,
Postquam flebilibus modis
Siluas currere mobiles,
Amnes stare coegerat,
Iunxitque intrepidum latus   10
Sæuis cerua leonibus,
Nec uisum timuit lepos
Iam cantu placidum canem.
Cum flagrantior intima
Feruor pectoris ureret   15
Nec qui cuncta subegerant
Mulcerent dominum modi,
Inmites superos querens
Infernas adiit domos.
Illic blanda sonantibus   20
Chordis carmina temperans
Quidquid præcipuis deæ
Matris fontibus hauserat,
Quod luctus dabat impotens,
Quod luctum geminans amor,   25
Deflet Tænara commouens,
El dulci ueniam prece
Vmbrarum dominos rogat.
Stupet tergeminus nouo

Captus carmine ianitor,   30
Quæ sontes agitant metu
Vltrices scelerum deæ
Iam mastæ lacrimis madent.
Non ixionium caput
Velox præcipitat rota,   35
Et longa site perditus
Spernit flumina Tantalus.
Vultur dum satur est modis,
Non traxit Tityi iecur.
Tandem "uincimur" arbiter   40
Vmbrarum miserans ait:
"Donamus comitem uiro
Emptam carmine coniugem.
Sed lex dona coerceat,
Ne, dum Tartara liqueret,   45
Fas sit lumina flectere."
Quis legem det amantibus?
Maior lex amor est sibi.
Heu noctis prope terminos
Orpheus Eurydicen suam   50
Vidit perdidit occidit.
Vos hæc fabula respicit
Quicumque in superum diem
Mentem ducere quæritis.
Nam qui tartareum in specus   55
Victus lumina flexerit,
Quidquid præcipuum trahit,
Perdit, dum uidet inferos.

Reprinted from Early English Text Society, original series, vol. 113 (London: K. Paul, Trench, Trübner & Co., 1899; Revised, 1931), by permission of the publisher.

Old English

ALFRED'S TRANSLATION,

Orpheus and Eurydice, 900

Hit gelamp gīo ðætte ān hearpere wæs on ðǣre ðīode ðe Ðrācia hātte, sīo wæs
on Grēca rīce; sē hearpere wæs swīðe ungefrǣglīce good, ðæs nama wæs Orfeus;
hē hæfde ān swīðe ǣnlīc wīf, sīo wæs hāten Eurudice. Ðā ongon mon secgan be
ðām hearpere, þæt hē meahte hearpian þæt sē wudu wagode, ond þā stānas hī
styredon for ðȳ swēge, ond wildu dīor ðǣr woldon tō irnan ond stondan swilce   5
hī tamu wǣren, swā stille, ðēah him men oððe hundas wið ēodon, ðæt hī hī nā ne
onscunedon. Ðā sǣdon hī þæt ðæs hearperes wīf sceolde ācwelan, ond hire sāule
mon sceolde lǣdan tō helle. Ða sceolde sē hearpere weorðan swā sārig, þæt hē
ne meahte ongemong ōðrum monnum bīon, ac tēah tō wuda, ond sæt on ðǣm
muntum, ǣgðer ge dæges ge nihtes, wēop ond hearpode, ðæt ðā wudas bifedon,   10
ond ðā ēa stōdon, ond nān heort ne onscunede nǣnne lēon, nē nān hara nǣnne
hund, nē nān nēat nyste nǣnne andan nē nǣnne ege tō ōðrum, for ðǣre mergðe
ðæs sōnes. Ða ðǣm hearpere ðā ðūhte ðæt hine nānes ðinges ne lyste on ðisse
worulde, ðā ðōhte hē ðæt hē wolde gesēcan helle godu, ond onginnan him
ōleccan mid his hearpan, ond biddan þæt hī him āgēafan eft his wif. Ðā hē ðā   15
ðider cōm, ðā sceolde cuman ðǣre helle hund ongēan hine, þæs nama wæs
Ceruerus, sē sceolde habban þrīo hēafdu, ond onfægnian mid his steorte, ond
plegian wið hine for his hearpunga. Ðā wæs ðǣr ēac swīðe egeslīc geatweard,
ðæs nama sceolde bīon Caron, sē hæfde ēac þrīo hēafdu, ond wæs swīðe
oreald. Ðā ongon sē hearpere hine biddan þæt hē hine gemundbyrde ðā hwīle   20
þe hē ðǣr wǣre, ond hine gesundne eft ðonan brōhte. Ðā gehēt hē him ðæt,
for ðǣm hē wæs oflyst ðæs seldcūðan sōnes. Ðā ēode hē furður oð hē gemētte
ðā graman gydena ðe folcise men hātað Parcas, ðā hī secgað ðæt on nānum men
nyten nāne āre, ac ǣlcum men wrecen be his gewyrhtum; þā hī secgað ðæt
wealden ǣlces mannes wyrde. Ða ongon hē biddan heora miltse; ða ongunnon   25
hī wēpan mid him. Ðā ēode hē furður, ond him urnon ealle hellwaran ongēan,
ond lǣddon hine tō hiora cyninge, ond ongunnon ealle sprecan mid him, ond
biddan ðæs ðe hē bæd. Ond þæt unstille hwēol ðe Ixīon wæs tō gebunden, Leuita
cyning, for his scylde, ðæt oðstōd for his hearpunga; ond Tantulus sē cyning,
ðe on ðisse worulde ungemetlīce gīfre wæs, ond him ðǣr ðæt ilce yfel filgde   30
ðǣre gīfernesse, hē gestilde. Ond sē vultor sceolde forlǣtan ðæt hē ne slāt
ðā lifre Tyties ðæs cyninges, ðe hine ǣr mid ðȳ wītnode; ond eall hellwara wītu
gestildon, ðā hwīle þe hē beforan ðam cyninge hearpode. Ðā hē ðā longe ond
longe hearpode, ðā cleopode sē hellwara cyning, ond cwæð: 'Wutun āgifan
ðǣm esne his wīf, for ðǣm hē hī hæfð geearnad mid his hearpunga.' Bebēad him   35

Reprinted from Sweet's *Anglo-Saxon Reader*, 14th ed., revised by C. T. Onions (Oxford: The
Clarendon Press, 1959), by permission of The Clarendon Press, Oxford.

ðā ðæt hē geare wisse, ðæt hē hine næfre under bæc ne besāwe, siððan hē
ðonanweard wǣre; ond sǣde, gif hē hine under bæc besāwe, ðæt hē sceolde
forlǣtan ðæt wīf. Ac ðā lufe mon mæg swīðe unēaðe oððe nā forbēodan: wēi
lā wēi! hwæt, Orpheus ðā lǣdde his wīf mid him, oð ðe hē cōm on þæt gemǣre
lēohtes ond ðīostro; ðā ēode þæt wīf æfter him. Ðā hē forð on ðæt lēoht cōm,   *40*
ðā beseah hē hine under bæc wið ðæs wīfes: ðā losade hīo him sōna. Ðās
lēasan spell lǣrað gehwylcne mon ðāra ðe wilnað helle ðīostro tō flīonne, ond tō
ðæs sōðan Godes līohte tō cumanne, ðæt hē hine ne besīo tō his ealdum yflum,
swā ðæt hē hī eft swā fullīce fullfremme swā hē hī ǣr dyde; for ðǣm swā hwā
swā mid fulle willan his mōd went tō ðǣm yflum ðe hē ǣr forlēt, ond hī ðonne   *45*
fullfremeð, ond hī him ðonne fullīce līciað, and hē hī næfre forlǣtan ne
þenceð, ðonne forlȳst hē eall his ǣrran good, būton hē hit eft gebēte.

Middle English
CHAUCER'S TRANSLATION,
Liber Tertius, Metrum 12, 1400

"*Felix qui potuit.*" Blisful is that man that may seen the clere welle of good!
Blisful is he that mai unbynden hym fro the boondes of the hevy erthe! The
poete of Trace (Orpheus), that whilom hadde ryght greet sorwe for the deth of
his wyf, aftir that he hadde makid by his weeply songes the wodes moevable to
renne, and hadde makid the ryveris to stonden stille, and hadde maked the   5
hertes and the hyndes to joynen dreedles here sydes to cruel lyouns (for to
herknen his song), and hadde maked that the hare was nat agast of the hound,
which was plesed by his song; so, whanne the moste ardaunt love of his wif
brende the entrayles of his breest, ne the songes that hadden overcomen alle
thinges ne mighten nat asswagen hir lord (orpheus), he pleynid hym of the   10
hevene goddis that weren cruel to hym. He wente hym to the houses of helle, and
ther he tempride his blaundysschinge songes by resounynge strenges, and spak
and song in wepynge al that evere he hadde resceyved and lavyd out of the
noble welles of his modir (Callyope), the goddesse. And he sang, with as mochel
as he myghte of wepynge, and with as moche as love, that doublide his sorwe,   15
myghte yeve hym and teche hym, and he commoevede the helle, and requyred
and bysoughte by swete preyere the lordes of soules in helle of relessynge (that
is to seyn, to yelden hym his wyf). Cerberus, the porter of helle, with his thre
hevedes was caught and al abasschid of the newe song. And the thre goddesses,
furiis and vengeresses of felonyes, that tormenten and agasten the soules by   20
anoy, woxen sorweful and sory, and wepyn teeris for pite. Tho was nat the heved
of Ixion ytormented by the overthrowynge wheel. And Tantalus, that was
destroied by the woodnesse of long thurst, despyseth the floodes to drynken.
The foul that highte voltor, that etith the stomak or the gyser of Tycius, is so
fulfild of his song that it nil eten ne tiren no more. At the laste the lord and juge 25
of soules was moevid to misericordes, and cryede: 'We ben overcomen,' quod
he; 'yyve we to Orpheus his wif to beren hym compaignye; he hath wel
ybought hire by his faire song and his ditee. But we wolen putten a lawe in this
and covenaunt in the yifte; that is to seyn that, til he be out of helle, yif he loke
byhynde hym, that his wyf schal comen ageyn unto us.' But what is he that may 30
yeven a lawe to loverys? Love is a grettere lawe and a strengere to hymself
(thanne any lawe that men mai yyeven). Allas! whanne Orpheus and his wyf
weren almost at the termes of the nyght (that is to seyn, at the laste boundes of
helle), Orpheus lokede abakward on Erudyce his wif, and lost hire, and was
deed. This fable apertenith to yow alle, whosoevere desireth or seketh to lede his 35

thought into the sovereyn day (that is to seyn, into cleernesse of sovereyn good). For whoso that evere be so overcomen that he ficche his eien into the put of helle (that is to seyn, whoso sette his thoughtes in erthly thinges), al that evere he hath drawen of the noble good celestial he lesith it, whanne he looketh the helles (that is to seyn, into lowe thinges of the erthe)."   *40*

Early Modern English
ELIZABETH I's TRANSLATION,
The Third Booke, XII, Myter, 1593

Blist, that may of Good
The fontaine Clire behold,
happy that Can Of waighty
Erthe the bondes to breake.
The Tracian profit wons   *5*
his wives funeralz wailing
Whan with sorows note
The wauering trees he moued,
And stedy rivers made,
And hind caused Join   *10*
Unfearing Sides to Lion fierce.
Nor hare did feare the Looke
Of Cruel dog so plised with Song,
Whan ferventar desir the inward
brest more burnt,   *15*
Nor Could the notes that al subdued
Pacefie ther Lord,
Of Ireful Godz Complaining
The helly house went to.
Ther faining verse   *20*
Tuning to Sounding Stringe
What he drew from springes
The greatest of Mother Godz,
What feable mone could Giue,
What doubled Love afourd,   *25*
by Wailes and hel doth stur
And with dulce suite pardon
Of darkenes Lorde besiche.
Wondar doth the thre hedded
Jailor amasid with unwonted verse,   *30*

Revenging Goddes of faultes
That wontid Gilty feare
Sorowing with teares bedewed thé were.
not Ixiones hed
The whirling while did turne   *35*
And lost with longue thirst
Tantalus riuers skornes.
The Vultur fild with notes,
Tityus livor tared not.
At last wailing Said the Juge   *40*
Of Shady place "we yeld;
To man we giue his wife for feere,
Won by his Song.
With this Law bound be the gift,
While in the Tartar thou bidest,   *45*
turne back thy looke thou must not."
but who to Loue giues Law?
for greatest Law his Love he made.
So night drawing to her ende,
Eurydicen his Oreus   *50*
Sawe, Lost, and killed.
this fable toucheth you
Who so doth seak to gide
To hiest day his mynd.
for who in helly Shade   *55*
Won man his yees doth bend,
What so he chifest held
In vewing hel hathe lost.
    Et Sic bene.[1]

Reprinted from Early English Text Society, original series, vol. 113 (London: K. Paul, Trench, Trübner & Co., 1899; Revised, 1931).
[1]This line is added by the Queen.

Modern English
RICHARD H. GREEN'S TRANSLATION,
Book Three, Poem 12, 1962

'Happy is he who can look into the shining spring of good; happy is he who can break the heavy chains of earth.

'Long ago the Thracian poet, Orpheus, mourned for his dead wife. With his sorrowful music he made the woodland dance and the rivers stand still. He made the fearful deer lie down bravely with the fierce lions; the rabbit no longer feared the dog quieted by his song. 5

'But as the sorrow within his breast burned more fiercely, that music which calmed all nature could not console its maker. Finding the gods unbending, he went to the regions of hell. There he sang sweet songs to the music of his harp, songs drawn from the noble fountains of his goddess mother, songs inspired by his powerless grief and the love which doubled his grief. 10

'Hell is moved to pity when, with his melodious prayer, he begs the favor of those shades. The three-headed guardian of the gate is paralyzed by that new song; and the Furies, avengers of crimes who torture guilty souls with fear, are touched and weep in pity. Ixion's head is not tormented by the swift wheel, and Tantalus, long maddened by his thirst, ignores the waters he now might drink. The vulture is filled by the melody and ignores the liver of Tityus. 15

'At last, the judge of souls, moved by pity, declares, "we are conquered. We return to this man his wife, his companion, purchased by his song. But our gift is bound by the condition that he must not look back until he has left hell." But who can give lovers a law? Love is a stronger law unto itself. As they approached the edge of night, Orpheus looked back at Eurydice, lost her, and died. 20

'This fable applies to all of you who seek to raise your minds to sovereign day. For whoever is conquered and turns his eyes to the pit of hell, looking into the inferno, loses all the excellence he has gained.' 25

Reprinted from Boethius, *The Consolation of Philosophy*, translated by Richard Green, copyright © 1962 by The Bobbs-Merrill Company, Inc., by permission of the Liberal Arts Press Division.

PARALLEL TEXTS OF THE NEW TESTAMENT
Matthew vi, 9–21

Gothic Text (translated by Bishop Ulfilas)
Ca., 360

9. Swa nu bidyaiþ yus, Atta unsar þu in himinam, weihnai namo þein;
10. Qimai þiudinassus þeins; wairþai wilya þeins swe in himina yah ana airþai;
11. Hlaif unsarana þana sinteinan gif uns himma daga;
12. Yah aflet una þatei skulans siyaima, swaswe yah weis afletam skulam unsaraim;
13. Yah ni briggais uns in fraistubnyai, ak lausei uns af þamma ubilin; unte þeina ist þiudangardi, yah mahts, yah wulþus in aiwins, Amen.
14. Unte yabai afletiþ mannam missadedins ize, afletiþ yah izwis atta izwar sa ufar himinam.
15. Iþyabai ni afletiþ mannam missadedins ize, ni þau atta izwar afletiþ missadedins izwaros.
16. Aþþan biþe fastaiþ, ni wairþaiþ swaswe þai liutans gaurain, frawardyand auk andwairþya seina, eigasaiwhaindau mannam fastandans; amen qiþa izwis, þatei andnemun mizdon seina.
17. Iþ þu fastands, salbo haubiþ þein, yah ludya þeina þwah,
18. Ei ni gasaiwhaizau mannam fastands, ak attin þeinamma þamma in fulhsnya, yah atta þeins saei saiwhiþ in fulhsnya, usgibiþ þus.
19. Ni huzdyaiþ izwis huzda ana airþai, þarei malo yah nidwa frawardieþ, yah þarei þiubos ufgraband yah hlifand;
20. Iþ huzdyaiþ izwis huzda in himina, þarei nih malo nih nidwa frawardeiþ, yah þarei þiubos ni ufgraband, nih stiland.
21. þarei auk ist huzd izwar, þaruh ist yah hairto izwar.

9. Eornostlīce gebiddaþ ēow þus Fæder ūre þū þe eart on heofonum, sīe þīn nama gehālgod.
10. Tōcume þīn rīce. Gewurþe þīn willa on eorþan swā swa on heofonum.
11. Ūrne daeghwǣmlican hlāf syle ūs tōdœg.
12. And forgyf ūs ūre gyltas swā swā we forgyfaþ ūrum gyltendum.
13. And ne gelǣd þū ūs on costnunge ac ālȳs ūs of yfcle.
14. Witodlīce gyf gē forgyfaþ mannum hyra synna, þonne forgyfþ ēower sē heofonlīca fæder ēow ēowre gyltas.
15. Gyf gē sōþlīce ne forgyfaþ mannum, ne ēower fæder ne forgyfþ ēow ēowre synna.
16. Sōþlīce þonne gē fæston, nellon gē wesan swylce lēase-licceteras, hīg fornymaþ hyra ansyna, þæt hīg æteowun mannum fæstende; sōþlīce ic secge eow, þæt hīg onfēngon hyra mede.
17. Dū sōþlīce þonne þū fæste, smȳra þīn heafod, and þweah þīne ansȳnc,
18. Dæt þū ne sȳ gesewen fram mannum fæstende, ac þīnum fæder þē ys on dȳglum, and þīn fæder þē gesyhþ on dȳglum, hyt āgylt þē.
19. Nellen gē gold-hordian ēow gold-hordas on eorþan, þær ōm and moþþe hit fornimþ, and þær þeofas hit delfaþ and forstelaþ;
20. Gold-hordiaþ ēow sōþlīce gold-hordas on heofenan, þær nador ōm ne moþþe hit ne fornimþ, and þær þeofas hit ne delfaþ, ne ne forstelaþ.
21. Wītodlīce þær þīn gold-hord is, þær is þīn heorte.

9. Forsothe thus ȝe shulen preyen, Oure fadir that art in heuenes, halwid be thi name;
10. Thy kyngdom cumme to; be thi wille don as in heuen and in erthe;
11. Ȝif to vs this day oure breed ouer other substaunce;
12. And forȝeue to vs oure dettis, as we forȝeue to oure dettours;
13. And leede vs nat in to temptacioun, but delyuere vs fro yuel. Amen.
14. Forsothe ȝif ȝee shulen forȝeuve to men her synnys, and ȝoure heuenly fadir shal forȝeue to ȝou ȝoure trespassis.
15. Sothely ȝif ȝee shulen forȝeue not to men, neither ȝoure fadir shal forȝeue to ȝou ȝoure synnes.
16. But when ȝee fasten, nyl ȝe be maad as ypocritis sorweful, for thei putten her facis out of kyndly termys, that their seme fastynge to men; trewly Y say to ȝou, thei han resseyued her meede.
17. But whan thou fastist, anoynte thin hede, and washe thi face,
18. That thou be nat seen fastynge to men, but to thi fadir that is in hidlis, and thi fadir seeth in hidlis, shal ȝeelde to thee.
19. Nyle ȝe tresoure to ȝou tresours in erthe, wher rust and mouȝthe distruyeth, and wher theeues deluen out and stelen;
20. But tresoure ȝee to ȝou tresouris in heuene, wher neither rust ne mouȝthe distruyeth, and wher theues deluen nat out, ne stelen.
21. Forsothe wher thi tresour is, there and thin herte is.

Early Modern English
TYNDALE, 1526

9. After thys maner there fore praye ye, O oure father which arte in heven, halowed be thy name;
10. Let thy kingdom come; thy wyll be fulfilled as well in erth as hit ys in heven;
11. Geve vs this daye oure dayly breade;
12. And forgeve vs oure treaspases, even as we forgeve them which trespas vs;
13. Loode vs not into temptacion, but delyvre vs ffrom yvell. Amen.
14. For and yff ye shall forgeve other men there trespases, youre father in heven shal also forgeve you.
15. But and ye wyll not forgeve men there trespases, no more shall youre father forgeve youre trespases.
16. Moreovre when ye faste, be not sad as the yporcrites are, for they disfigure there faces, that hit myght apere vnto men that they faste; verely Y say vnto you, they have there rewarde.
17. But thou when thou fastest, annoynte thyne heed, and washe thy face,
18. That it appere nott vnto men howe that thou fastest, but vnto thy father which is in secrete, and thy father which seith in secret, shall rewarde the openly.
19. Gaddre not treasure together on erth, where rust and mothes corrupte, and where theves breake through and steale;
20. But gaddre ye treasure togedder in heven, where nether rust nor mothes corrupte, and wher theves nether breake vp, nor yet steale.
21. For whearesoever youre treasure ys, ther are youre hertes also.

MONSIGNOR KNOX, 1944

This, then, is to be your prayer, Our Father, who art in heaven, hallowed be thy name; thy kingdom come; thy will be done, on earth as it is in heaven; give us this day our daily bread;[1] and forgive us our trespasses, as we forgive them that trespass against us; and lead us not into temptation, but deliver us from evil. Amen. Your heavenly Father will forgive you your transgressions, if you   *5* forgive your fellow-men theirs; if you do not forgive them, your heavenly Father will not forgive your transgressions either. (vv. 9–15)

Again, when you fast, do not shew it by gloomy looks, as the hypocrites do. They make their faces unsightly, so that men can see they are fasting; believe me, they have their reward already. But do thou, at thy times of fasting, anoint thy   *10* head and wash thy face, so that thy fast may not be known to men, but to thy Father who dwells in secret; and then thy Father, who sees what is done in secret, will reward thee. (vv. 16–18)

Do not lay up treasures for yourselves on earth, where there is moth and rust to consume it, where there are thieves to break in and steal it; lay up   *15* treasures for yourselves in heaven, where there is no moth or rust to consume it, no thieves to break in and steal. Where your treasure-house is, there your heart is too. (vv. 19–21)

The scripture quotations are in the translation of Monsignor Ronald Knox, copyright 1944, 1948, and 1950, Sheed & Ward, Inc., New York, with the kind permission of his Eminence the Cardinal Archbishop of Westminster.

[1]'Daily': the Latin here (but not in Lk. II. 3) coins the word *supersubstantialis,* which has sometimes been understood as a direct reference to the Holy Eucharist.

Modern English
REVISED STANDARD VERSION, 1952

9. Pray then like this:
    Our Father who art in heaven,
    Hallowed by thy name.
10. Thy kingdom come,
    Thy will be done,
      On Earth as it is in heaven.
11. Give us this day our daily bread;[1]
12. And forgive us our debts,
      As we also have forgiven our debtors;
13. And lead us not into temptation,
      But deliver us from evil.[2]
14. For if you forgive men their trespasses, your heavenly Father also will forgive you;
15. but if you do not forgive men their trespasses, neither will your Father forgive your trespasses.
16. And when you fast, do not look dismal, like the hypocrites, for they disfigure their faces that their fasting may be seen by men. Truly, I say to you, they have their reward.
17. But when you fast, anoint your head and wash your face,
18. that your fasting may not be seen by men but by your Father who is in secret; and your Father who sees in secret will reward you.
19. Do not lay up for yourselves treasures on earth, where moths and rust[3] consume and where thieves break in and steal,
20. but lay up for yourselves treasures in heaven, where neither moth nor rust[4] consumes and where thieves do not break in and steal.
21. For where your treasure is, there will your heart be also.

QUESTION

In Exercise 7, using a sample of Chaucer's prose to represent the English language of 1400, you prepared a paper evaluating prose writing. That exercise might now be regarded as a type of "mid-way" demonstration, where you brought together your

[1]Or—our bread for the morrow
[2]Or—the evil one. Other authorities, some ancient, add, in some form—For thine is the kingdom and the power and the glory, for ever. Amen.
[3]Or—worm
[4]Or—worm

observations about the changes in the language from its beginning to a point roughly half way through its development until now. Now you can pick up those earlier conclusions and complete your general survey of the history of English. These texts show how writers at different times, from earliest to contemporary, have dealt with the same material, have used the resources of their language—the English of their time—to prepare translations adequate for their age, sufficient to the needs of audiences of their generation. These texts are, in short, an actual display, in brief compass, of the history and development of the English language. They constitute a restricted, manageable body of material which may serve as the base for either written reports or class discussions to draw out, as you employ all the techniques you have learned, statements about the development of your language.